I Need Answers

Deacon Dawit Muluneh

I Need Answers

Copyright © 2019 by Dawit Muluneh. All rights reserved. No portion of this book may be reproduced, stored in a retrieval system, or transmitted in any form or by any means, except for brief quotations in printed reviews, without prior permission of Dawit Muluneh. Requests may be submitted by email: dawitmuluneh@gmail.com.

Unless otherwise indicated, all Scripture quotations are taken from the *Holy Bible*, New Living Translation, copyright © 1996, 2004, 2015 by Tyndale House Foundation. Used by permission of Tyndale House Publishers, Inc., Carol Stream, Illinois 60188. All rights reserved.

Scripture quotations marked NIV taken from THE HOLY BIBLE, NEW INTERNATIONAL VERSION®, Copyright © 1973, 1978, 1984, 2011 by Biblica, Inc.® Used by permission. All rights reserved worldwide.

Scripture quotations marked NKJV taken from the New King James Version®. Copyright © 1982 by Thomas Nelson. Used by permission. All rights reserved.

Scripture quotations marked WE taken from the Worldwide English (New Testament). © 1969, 1971, 1996, 1998 by SOON Educational Publications, Willington, Derby, DE65 6BN, England. All rights reserved.

Editing, cover design, and page formatting by ChristianEditingServices.com

Interior illustrations by Devin Schmidt of ChristianEditingServices.com.

Illustrations copyright © 2019 by Devin Schmidt.

I dedicate this book to the Young Orthodox Tewahedo Christians (YOTC), who have relentlessly supported me throughout the process of writing this book. As we say in YOTC, "We are all a family!" I have been blessed to see that saying demonstrated since the beginning of this journey. May God bless us with many more years together.

Contents

Acknowledgments   7

Introduction   11

    Chapter1:   I Just Don't Get It!   23

    Chapter2:   Do I Have to Go to Church?   29

    Chapter3:   Jesus Is Everywhere!   46

    Chapter4:   Getting Right with God   59

    Chapter5:   Fasting Time . . . Again?   71

    Chapter6:   The Birds and the Bees   83

    Chapter7:   I Was Born This Way   102

    Chapter8:   The Struggle Is Real   113

    Chapter9:   Parents Are from Mars and Children Are from Venus   125

    Chapter10:   I Wanna Be a Deacon . . . I Think   141

    Chapter11:   What's Next?   159

FAQ'S for the New Church-Goer   167

Resources   189

Acknowledgments

I want to first thank God for all He has done in my life! I am nothing without Him and the love He gives me. From the beginning to the end, He has not left me. May all glory be given to Him.

I offer my deepest gratitude and appreciation to your grace, Bitsu Abune Fanuel. It is truly a blessing to know we have a father like you in our generation. You took the time to go through this book in its initial stages and guide me throughout this process. The encouragement and guidelines you provided were vital for me. May God give you the grace of your spirit.

Qomos Abba Philipos, I have no words to thank you. You not only taught me about Christianity but also showed me what it looks like. Each day you exemplify what it means to live the life of a Christian and live out your responsibilities as both a priest and a monk. May God increase your services and be with you forever.

Wherever you are, my beloved Kine teacher Memhir Hawaz from Debrelibanos, I cannot thank you enough for what you have done for me. Without looking down on me, you accepted me into the monastery and invested your energy in me. Most of all, taking time away from the few hours of sleep you would get, you spent extra time with me teaching me Kine and encouraging me to learn. You were a father, a brother, a teacher, and so much more. May God be with you in all your journey! And may the intercession of our father Tekelehaymanot never leave your side!

Liqetebet Tibeb Yiheyis, I honestly have no words to thank you for all you have done for me. When we first met, I was barely able to recognize the Ethiopic letters and alphabets. You took time from your busy schedule to sit with me several times a week making sure I was able to read and pronounce each word properly. You never gave up on me or looked down on me. When I went to Debre Libanos, this foundation enabled me to transition smoothly to the Kine school. I am thankful to have a spiritual father like you in my life. May God increase your services and may the intercession of the archangel Michael be with you.

Memhir Hizkias Mamo, I am who I am because God has worked through you. When it comes to service, you have pushed my limits beyond measure. Like a Solomonic father "not sparing the rod," you have guided me throughout my life since we crossed paths nearly a decade ago. Your dedication for the youth and love for the Church are truly an inspiration. I have never seen anyone work as hard as you do. May the intercession of St. Mary never leave your side.

ACKNOWLEDGEMENTS

Hohite Semay St. Mary Ethiopian Orthodox Tewahido Church (Vancouver, Canada), I greatly appreciate the support you have given me during the writing of this book. Everyone's hard work and dedication to the youth is truly inspirational. May your services be multiplied and may you see the fruits of your hard work.

I want to give deepest gratitude to the community in Taylor, Texas, for your unwavering support throughout this process. Without your support I would not have been able to make it this far. I can honestly say, doing Bible study sessions with you has been a true blessing. May God give us more years to come.

I also want to thank God for giving me wonderful parents to teach me about my faith. Mom, you are still available to answer questions I may have. You continue to help me grow in my spiritual life and are one of my favorite and best mentors! Dad, you have been my number-one supporter. Even in those times when I did not believe in myself, you have always been there to remind me of the talents God has given me. In the making of this book, you were there every step of the way giving me the guidelines I needed and the support that is greatly appreciated. I also am thankful for having an older brother to whom I can always go for advice. Dear Brother, like mom and dad, you are always encouraging me and inspiring me to challenge myself and do bigger and better things.

I believe God has always communicated to me through the amazing spiritual mentors He has placed in my life. Not only do they know the teachings of the Church thoroughly, but they also live the life of Christianity according to the same teachings they give me.

Special thanks you, my Sunday school students. You have supported me in this process of publishing this book. It is humbling to know the same young kids I once mentored are now all grown up and able to assist me in this project. One of the greatest joys I have is in your success in your personal, professional, and spiritual lives. You all make me so proud. I am honored to have been—and still continue to be—your Sunday school teacher.

Last but definitely not least, I want to thank my amazing friends who have supported me throughout this process. Whether it was giving me new ideas and perspectives or taking the time to give me feedback, I am thankful to have all of you in my life.

Keep me in your prayers: *Tsirste-medhin.*

Thank you!

INTRODUCTION

In the Name of the Father, Son, and Holy Spirit One God, Amen

I grew up in the Ethiopian Orthodox Tewhido Church in the city of Addis Ababa, the capital of Ethiopia. The earliest memories I have of Ethiopia involve my mom holding my hand and the two of us running as fast as we could toward the gate of the church as the early service bells were being struck. Going to church was a part of my weekly routine, as it was with most Ethiopians; however, I especially remember the Sunday mornings. I recall the liturgy services, the abundance of people during holidays, the drums—the *kabero*—and the singing of hymns. Although I was a child and slept through much of the liturgy, the energy of the drumbeats and the singing of the hymns woke me, both literally and spiritually. Even though I appreciated some of it, I did not understand parts of the service and found much of it uninteresting. Even so, although I did not realize it back then, I began falling in love with the Church.

I NEED ANSWERS

My involvement with the Church began to grow once I came to America at the age of seven when my family and I moved to Arlington, Virginia. We found our new church home, and the difference was striking. To my surprise, the church in America had a youth program. For the first time I seemed to have a place in the Church. Consequently, I began to thoroughly enjoy the services—especially the liturgy. Sunday officially became my favorite day of the week. I recall we would perform plays, sing *mezmures*, and eventually even study *wereb*—the spiritual hymns! Thus, for the for first time in my life I felt excited to be at church.

I owe much of my excitement to my Sunday school teacher, Shimeles. I still remember being greeted by him for the first time when I walked into the Sunday school classroom at Debre Selam Mariam Church in D.C. over twenty years ago. He was extremely delighted to meet my brother and me, and he immediately made us feel welcome. For the next ten years Shimeles played the role of a brother, mentor, teacher, and so much more. I was mesmerized by how many *mezmures* he was able to teach us each week. He would call us throughout the week to make sure we were studying the lyrics and have us practice before we finally performed on Sunday before the congregation. I remember all the plays he would write and have us present before our parents. Throughout this process, all of us students were able to come together and create a bond that would last for years. More than anything else, I am thankful for the love Shimeles gave us. I remember one day when we were unable to come to church, he came all the way to our house to pick up my brother and me. His constant dedication to teach and his love for the students created a platform for hundreds of students to keep coming to church weekly.

INTRODUCTION

This wonderful chapter of my Sunday school life abruptly came to a halt in my high school days when Shimeles was no longer able to teach us regularly as he moved on to the next chapter of his life. His frequent absence had a profound impact on the youth at the church. Suddenly hundreds of students, primarily English speakers, would come to church and there was no one to teach them. Other Sunday school teachers attempted to come and teach, but they were primarily Amharic speakers and were unable to connect with the students. The students often complained that they could not connect with the teachings of the Church; as a result, they began to ask why they had to continue attending the Ethiopian Orthodox Tehwahedo Church—a church where they could not relate or speak the language. With no one there to answer their urgent questions, they simply stopped coming.

This saddened me because I loved my church. I could not stand to watch as students left the church in massive numbers, so I took it upon myself to do something about it. I was only seventeen years old and had no formal training or guidance in teaching, yet one Sunday morning I found myself standing before my peers as I began conducting a Sunday school class. I wish I could say I started this because of a genuine interest in serving God, but that could not be farther from the truth. It started one particular Sunday during the time Shimeles was able to teach less and less because of his other commitments. He was late to the Sunday class that day and the students were getting a bit too rowdy. I seized this opportunity to get up before the class and pretend to be the teacher. Truthfully, I was simply mocking him. It was supposed to be a fun, innocent joke among the students. But as I stood there mocking, Shimeles walked in! You can imagine my shock and the fear on my face. I am so glad he did not hear anything I had said prior to his arrival. I quickly got off the podium, but he was adamant about my continuing to teach. I remember feeling sick to my stomach. I did not know what to say. I did a few "ums" and "uhs" for a while and thought about the only subject I knew, Adam and Eve. When I got down, Shimeles stood up and praised me for my ability to take charge when he was gone—not knowing my true intentions. Over time I was given more responsibility around the Sunday school class. When I look back now, I realize that particular Sunday morning was the beginning of a new chapter God was writing in my life.

For the next few years I spent my Sunday mornings teaching classes. Although I considered it an immense blessing to be a part of this service, I remember the great frustration I felt at the time. Without any lesson plans or guidance from others, I found myself in the middle of doing something without adequate skill sets to succeed. This was the first time I was able to see how few resources were made available for someone like me. I wanted greatly to understand the teachings of the Ethiopian Orthodox Tewahedo Church, yet there were no books, lessons, teachers, or guidelines to help me. Even with these limitations, I was amazed to see the young kids continuing to come to church ready to learn every Sunday morning. Thus, I kept on coming too. This experience taught me a major lesson. I discovered that the new generation within our church is extremely interested and willing to learn about the Church, yet they must have someone to connect with. That is, they have to have someone who is cross-cultural to connect with, someone who understands the culture in both Ethiopia and America.

My teaching days came to a temporary end when I went to college. The first few months of college were difficult for me since this was the first time in my life when I could not go to church every Sunday. Many college students get homesick the first year of college, but I was "church sick." I recall that when I really wanted to sing *mezmures*, I would hide in the bathroom and begin singing, yet I was embarrassed to think that my college friends would make fun of me if they heard me.

Few of my college friends were Ethiopian, let alone part of the Ethiopian Orthodox Tewhedo Church. Eventually I became more like them as I found it difficult to balance the extremely opposing worlds of the church life and college life. The struggle was exhausting, and I decided to submit to the college life. I stopped doing my daily prayers, singing *mezmure,* and listening to sermons. I became detached from the church. I went from really missing my church the first few months of college to avoiding church—even when I was at home with my parents.

After a long time of being away, I finally decided to go back to my home church to visit my Sunday school students. I was heartbroken to find none of my students in the class. Instead, I was greeted by a new set of students who had replaced them. Later on I learned that many of my Sunday school students had departed from the church out of frustration from not being able to understand the teachings. Once again, without anyone being able to properly answer their questions about the Church in a manner (and in a language) they could understand, they simply stopped coming. This issue was further complicated by the reality that no system was put in place to follow up with the status of the youth ministry. That is to say, many members of the Ethiopian Orthodox Tewahedo Church responded to the problem of the youth abandoning the Church by simply throwing up their hands as a sign of defeat without implementing solutions to the problem.

As I mentioned, no leaders within the church were assigned to follow up with students as they went away to college. The transition to college for the youth of the church was quite difficult and wrought with serious questions going unanswered. They were sent off to school without the proper ammunition needed to fight off the great struggles they would face.

Sad to say, this is still the reality of many young adults today. I have talked to countless young people who are ready to confess their sins and appear before a priest but never do so because they don't know how to articulate their ideas in Amharic. The idea of confession is already hard as it is, especially for someone who grew up in this country. We are asking these young people to tell their deepest secrets to a person they just met. And as if this weren't intimidating already, we are asking them to do it in a language they barely know! In the midst of battling their biggest spiritual warfare, sexual temptation, they are also faced with the task of defending their faith. I remember my college days as my roommates and I sat around talking about various issues we found interesting. One topic that seemed to resurface often was religion. While I described our tradition, starting from what we eat to how we worship, the common response was "Why do you do these things?" I would often have no answer to give and felt ashamed for not being able to explain the practices of my church.

Once again, this is the reality of many college students today. When they go away to college, their friends see them fasting, waking up early in the morning to do Kidase, and wearing white clothes on Sunday mornings. The friends ask

INTRODUCTION

why they are doing what they are doing. If they are unable to answer, they often feel ridiculed and frustrated. Their friends' questions slowly develop into their own. "Why do I have to fast all these days?" "Why do I have to wake up in the morning to go to church?" "Why do I have to wear white on Sundays?" If they are unable to get answers to these questions, they stop coming to church altogether. Once again, this is the reality of thousands of kids throughout the country. Teaching kids Amharic will not teach them how to fight sexual temptations in college. Learning Amharic will not help them answer the questions they face when they go away to college. Although there are many benefits for kids to learn Amharic, the focus should be on the spiritual growth of the students rather than what language they speak. As a church we have to learn how to teach the students about their faith in the language they understand.

For several years now the norm for Sunday school has been teaching students the alphabet of the Ethiopian language and at most getting them to sing *mezmures* on Sundays. This method has failed hundreds if not thousands of kids across the country. We have a serious epidemic in the Church. If we want to ensure that there is a future generation who can take over this church, we must come up with a method to teach our children about their faith. Currently they are set up to fail. Without constant reminders of the Christian teachings that were instilled in them as children, they fall away from the Church. Seeing this great problem and experiencing it firsthand, I recommitted myself to my church. Although doing so was difficult because I was away at college, I recommitted also to the Sunday school.

Once I graduated from college, I was able to dedicate more time to this task. To prepare myself more fully for teaching

Sunday school, I found myself attending many Bible studies to increase my knowledge about the Orthodox Church. At one of these Bible studies the following question was posed to me by one of the most honorable priests I know, Abba Philipos: "Is Orthodoxy in America hard or easy?" I was quick to respond: "HARD!" I proceeded to explain my position by referencing all the additional temptations one may endure in America compared with in Ethiopia. I spoke passionately about the language barrier, the cultural differences, and the temptations of a young adult constantly faced with ideas and concepts that appear to go against the teachings of Christ. As I was making these points, the priest nodded his head as a sign of agreement. When I saw his approval, I was happy to know that I got the answer "right."

Several weeks later a new person who had grown up in Ethiopia joined the Bible study program. The priest asked him the same question. This time the person adamantly protested that Orthodoxy in America was easy. His reasoning was that in Ethiopia people are expected to pray longer, fast all the time, and follow all the guidelines of the Church. To my surprise, however, the priest gave the same nod of approval he had given me a few weeks prior. I was left with more questions than answers. Who was right?

Over the next few years I saw the priest asking the same question to a considerable number of people with varying backgrounds and give the same nod of approval regardless of the answers they gave. As I sat there and listened to each person's answer followed with justification for their answer, I began to understand a few things. First, I learned there was no "right" answer. More importantly, people's upbringing influenced the answer they gave. Those who grew up in Ethiopia saw Orthodoxy in America as easy,

INTRODUCTION

often explaining the strict guidelines followed in Ethiopia were not practiced here in America. On the other hand, those who had assimilated into the American culture expressed their concerns regarding the challenges they faced within the Orthodox Church.

Sadly, very little attention has been given to the concerns of these American-assimilated Ethiopians. Few attempts have been made to rectify the issues, which brings me to the second thing I learned from the priest in the Bible study: a platform needs to be created to address the concerns of those who have grown up in North America. Some strongly resist this idea since they assume it creates a division within the Church. For example, I once proposed having two Sunday schools: one in Amharic and the other in English. As a result, I was accused of attempting to divide the Church. But the reality is this: through this division the Church can become more unified. Churches suffer growing pains, and there is a longstanding tradition of these types of controversies. Did not Saint Paul write various letters to specific churches addressing the relevant issues each church had, ultimately offering solutions to their issues? I am no Saint Paul, but I have found myself offering solutions to the specific problems raised by the Orthodox community in America.

As I continued to ponder these issues, I began to take even more time to learn about the beautiful teachings of the Church. I was left in awe at how amazing and beautiful the teachings of our church are. I wanted to share everything I learned with my Sunday school students, and I guess my enthusiasm was contagious. Sure, I was teaching the students in English, and this was considered a radical move; however, this way they were easily able to understand the teachings of the Church. As a result, they fell in love with the Church just as I had done!

Suddenly Sunday classes were not enough! My students demanded additional class periods throughout the week. After listening to their pleas, I started Bible study sessions on Friday nights for young adults between the ages of sixteen and twenty-one. These brave souls were willing to sacrifice their Friday nights to learn about their church. How wonderful! Some Friday nights we would stay at the church until midnight! It is clear that this was not the work of me but rather the work of God.

I have learned that the next generation is eager to know more about orthodoxy. All they need is an opportunity to learn in the language they understand. For example, one of the many students I have taught was a young boy named Kaleab. He must have been sixteen or seventeen when I first met him. At the time, he was mixed up with a group of troubled students. He had already started experimenting with drugs and was on a path not conducive to his spiritual life. Nonetheless, he was always interested in learning about the Church. He was one of the people who demanded extra days to conduct Bible study. Because he was able to get his questions answered, he kept coming to church every Sunday. In college he was given the task of mentoring younger kids and eventually started teaching Sunday school. Today Kaleab has graduated from college and is serving this church fervently. Because of the foundation Sunday school provided, he learned about the Church and was able to continue growing in it. His story demonstrates that once students are given a platform for learning, they end up being devoted Christians who continue to serve their church.

Over the next few years I traveled across the country to various cities to teach about Orthodoxy in English. During

INTRODUCTION

this period I met many wonderful young adults with the same eagerness and enthusiasm for learning as those students in my hometown. Many of these young adults expressed feelings of being detached from the Church and not being able to relate to it simply because of the language barrier. I found this issue of detachment throughout the country. In each place I visited, I made sure to listen to the concerns and questions the young people had. I used patience and discernment, and I took time to read the holy books of our forefathers with them. I sat down with the scholars of the Church to find fitting answers. Thus, it has taken a unified team within the Orthodox community to tackle the problem of detachment. We have made much progress in offering solutions to this problem. Seeing that many other people with similar problems could benefit from some of the dialogues that have taken place with my students, church scholars, and members of the Church, I decided to write this book.

Each chapter within this book addresses a specific question. Within the chapter a number of sub-questions related to the overall theme of the chapter are raised. Although the delivery and style of writing may be unique, the content of the book (the answers to the questions) are found in the holy books of our church. I must point out that I have done my best to rule out my own subjectivity. That is, I did not write this book simply to share my personal opinions with the readers. Instead, I translated the teachings of our forefathers into English. These translations are presented it in a way that can be understood by those who grew up outside Ethiopia. I pray and hope that those who read this book can finally see how beautiful and rich our Church truly is.

CHAPTER 1

I Just Don't Get It!

The Ethiopian Orthodox Church is two thousand years old! Think about it. For over two thousand years people have been attending this church, making it one of the oldest Christian churches in the world. This is a church with rich history, which can be traced back to the time of the Queen of Sheba and her journey to King Solomon (1 Kings 10). In fact, the Ethiopian Orthodox Tewhedo Church proudly gained its first member only a year after Christ's resurrection, as recorded in Acts 8:26–40. There are a multitude of reasons for this church's longevity, but have you really ever wondered why so many people are dedicated to it? There must be a good reason after all.

If your parents are the typical Habesha parents, you can probably recall those dreadful Sunday mornings waking up to the distressing voice of your mom. Yes, we all love our mamas, but our love slightly diminishes on Sunday mornings when it is time to get out of bed. In all honesty, the main reason your parents are nagging you to go to church early in the mornings is because being in church is their primary source of joy and happiness. And yes, hundreds of thousands of faithful Orthodox Christians around the world feel the same way! However, if you are reading this book, you may not feel the same excitement for the Church as so many others do. Have you ever been to an Ethiopian Orthodox Church and felt as if you didn't know what was going on? Are you crazy—or is everybody else crazy?

For starters, you are not alone! Nearly hundreds if not thousands of smart young people just like you feel—*exactly* the same way. I was one of them, and this is one reason I am writing this book. Also, I am a youth Sunday school teacher for the Ethiopian Orthodox Church and get a chance to travel all over the country and meet many parents and young people. No matter where I go, I see similar problems almost everywhere. If I had to pinpoint the most frequent problem I hear about during my travels, it is that the parents feel as if their children are falling away from the Church; in turn, the kids feel as though their parents are putting lots of pressure on them. Does this sound familiar?

Think about it for a second. This pressure doesn't mean your parents are monsters or that there is something wrong with your family. It just means your parents and you have a difference of opinion when it comes to the Church. This is why I am here: I seek to help you and your parents see eye to eye since leaving the Church has probably crossed your mind a time or two. Or you may have already left the Church. Before you entirely give up on the Ethiopian Orthodox Church, remember to ask yourself how a church was able to survive this long. Two thousand years is a very long time, friends.

I JUST DON'T GET IT!

Obviously the Church has something to offer, but what? Let's look at it this way: the video game Fortnite has over 250 million players worldwide. So what about this game draws the attention of so many young people? Even if you are not interested in playing video games, at the very least you should be curious to know why so many people are drawn to this one. We can surmise this: the game has something good to offer. Now we all know video games are controversial, so let's look at this way: the game fulfills some sort of need in the lives of the people who play it. The same thing is true with the Church: the fifty million people who make up the Ethiopian Orthodox Church are getting their needs fulfilled. Plus, this has been going on for over two thousand years! Even if you have no desire to be a follower of the Ethiopian Orthodox Church, you should invest some time to see why all these people have been going to church day after day and week after week for the last two thousand years. As you do this, remember to keep asking this: What are people getting out of the Church?

I know what you are thinking. If the Church has so many great things to offer, why don't I get anything good out of it? I don't know if you have noticed, but the Ethiopian Orthodox Church speaks primarily . . . wait for it, wait for it . . . Amharic! If you grew up in America, you are likely to be an English speaker. Even if you can manage to understand what your grandma says to you when you go to Ethiopia, you are likely to understand an English sermon better than an Amharic one. Also, let's not forget the liturgy (Kidase) is often done in Ge'ez.

Until the last decade or so there was no reason for the Ethiopian Church to use English for services and sermons because many of her congregations were non-English speakers. But times have changed, and the Church is now recognizing this change. You may have recognized attempts to make church services more English friendly in the past few years. In fact, some Ethiopian Orthodox churches have already started providing English services. The language problem is slowly being fixed.

Language is not the only problem, however. Compared with the prior generation, this generation appears to be changing the way to practice faith. For example, people in our parents' generation were strong in their faith without needing much knowledge or evidence. Our parents believed in what they were told and trusted the Church. Questioning their faith was seen as a sign of having weak faith. On the other hand, we in the current generations (known as millennials and Generation Z) ask a lot of questions. That is, we want an explanation for everything! If someone is going to ask us to take off our shoes, we ask why. If we are told to fast, we ask why. If someone dares interrupt our beauty sleep on Sunday mornings, we demand an explanation.

The more I have thought about it, the more I have learned to understand that in their own way each respective generation benefits the other. The style of our parents' generation creates a type of faith that is strong and unshakable. However, this form of following what you are told without questioning simply does not work for the new generations. Millennials and Z'ers need to understand the meaning behind all the things we are doing.

The good news is that in this book I will attempt to unveil all the hidden meanings and start answering the "why" questions. From the vantage point of a person who grew up in America, it will address some key questions about the Ethiopian Orthodox Church. Some topics may be controversial while others might be uncomfortable to read. However you feel about what you read, you will at least be able to understand the reasoning behind why the Church does what it does.

Whether your parents are forcing you to read this book or someone recommended it to you or you found it yourself, try to read it with an open mind. Remember: many people are rooting for you—not just your parents but also a multitude of angels are waiting with excitement for you to come to church every Sunday. All the angels gather together and have a big feast when someone comes back to the Church. But most of all, God is looking down on you. He loves you very much and the Church is a great gift from Him to us. He is happy when we use His gift. Finally, as you read remember to have faith that you will come across something that will help you understand the Church better. If you open your heart and allow God to come in, He will lead you to a place where you can find an abundance of joy and happiness. Come, let us see what discoveries you will find about the Church!

Challenge: Pray the following prayer: "God, I ask You to lead me toward the truth. Help me lean on Your guidance instead of my understanding. Guide me, lead me, show me the way. I will follow!"

Discussion Questions

1. What are the biggest questions you have about the Ethiopian Orthodox Church?

2. Describe your experience within the Church. Is your family Orthodox Tewahedo?

3. Describe your last experience attending an Ethiopian Orthodox Tewahedo Church. What were the positives and negatives?

4. Do you find being a member of this church easy or hard? What is easy or hard about it?

5. Do you think many youths attend the Ethiopian Orthodox Church? Why do you think that is?

CHAPTER 2

Do I Have to Go to Church?

What Is a Church?

The word *church* in English doesn't have the same effect as it does in Amharic. The Amharic word for *church* is ቤተክርስቲያን (*betäkərətiyanə*). This word is the product of two words meshed into one: ቤት (*betə*), which means "house," and ክርስቲያን (*kərətiyanə*), which means "Christians." Putting these words together results in the term *house of Christians*. What we call the church is meant to serve us as our personal home!

Even in your personal home you have a room designated for specific things, right? For example, your bedroom is reserved for your bed, and your living room is meant for you to "live" or just hang out in. In the same way, the house of Christians is reserved for a specific purpose. So when Christians ask if they really need to go to church, they are in essence asking, "Do I really need to go home?" As you know, humans must have food, clothing, and shelter to survive. Therefore, the answer is an overwhelming *yes*. A Christian who refuses to go to church is like a rich kid with a big house who chooses to be homeless. By the way, if I had a mic, this would be the time to drop it . . .

#micdrop

The Church Is a Place Where We Receive Gifts

One person who played a major role in my spiritual growth is Abba Philipos. I can honestly say that he not only taught me about Christianity but also showed me how to live it. That is why I was so thankful when he gave me a cross he had purchased from Ethiopia. I already had many crosses around the house, most of them set to the side, but this cross meant the world to me because I greatly admire him. I placed the cross inside my car and often held on to it while I was driving. I know—it's not the safest thing to do, but the point is that I was able to appreciate the gift because I appreciate the person who gave it to me. I tell you this because I know of a place where you can receive cherished gifts every day.

No, you are not dreaming. The Church is a place where you can receive gift after gift every time you go even though it's not your birthday! Before we go any further in this discussion about the gifts, let me ask you a question: What kinds of things do you thank Jesus for? Most people will list their parents, siblings (even if you don't always like them), friends, house, food, and most of all Fortnite! Now, although these are definitely things we should be thankful for, there are much bigger things to give thanks for—namely that our Lord and Savior, Jesus Christ, came to this world and died for you and me!

You may be thinking, "So what?" Let me fill you in. Through His death Jesus left all of us an abundance of gifts. We receive these gifts through something we call "sacraments." These sacraments provide access to the gifts our Lord Jesus Christ left for us. Think of it this way: Imagine your parents are rich. I don't mean the kind of rich like they own a BMW but the kind of rich where they have private jets. Now, that's rich! Many such wealthy families leave their children a trust fund that allows their kids to access the money their parents leave them once they grow up. That money is already set aside for the children to claim, yet in order to claim the money that is legally theirs, they have to go to a bank to receive it. The bank is the means by which the heirs can access the money—the gift—left for them. In the same way, the Church is the bank where we are able to access the gifts Jesus has left for us. But here is the thing: these gifts—what we call the Seven Sacraments—are administered *only* within the Church. You cannot receive them anywhere else. Thus, if you do not go to church, you miss out on your chance to receive some pretty awesome gifts.[1]

---

1 It is also worth noting that these are not simple gifts we can live without—they are essential gifts. They are gifts that enable us to go to the kingdom of heaven. They are gifts that allow us to be in communion with Christ Jesus. These are gifts that open the gates to the kingdom of heaven. We should not look at them with simplicity but should approach them with the upmost reverence.

The Church Is a Place Where We Remember God's Name

In addition to being a place to receive gifts, the Church is a place where God's name is remembered. God spoke the following to Moses:

> "Build for me an altar made of earth, and offer your sacrifices to me—your burnt offerings and peace offerings, your sheep and goats, and your cattle. Build my altar wherever I cause my name to be remembered, and I will come to you and bless you." (Exodus 20:24)

This means the desire to have a special place dedicated to honoring and worshiping God was not the will of man but the will of God. If we truly want to obey Him, then we must be sure to follow His request and dedicate a special altar to remember His name.

But it doesn't end there. After Solomon built a temple, God responded to him by saying, "For I have chosen this Temple and set it apart to be holy—a place where my name will be honored forever. I will always watch over it, for it is dear to my heart" (2 Chronicles 7:16). God specifically set aside that particular place over other places by saying "this Temple." When we follow God's instructions and remember His name on the altar, we get blessings from God.

Now you may be thinking, "Isn't this in the Old Testament? Last time I checked we follow the New Testament. Jesus died for me so I don't need to worry about this stuff." Well, before you come to this conclusion, consider the following verse from the New Testament:

> He took some bread and gave thanks to God for it. Then he broke it in pieces and gave it to the disciples, saying, "This is my body, which is given for you. Do this in remembrance of me." After supper he took another cup of wine and said, "This cup is the new covenant between God and his people—an agreement confirmed with my blood, which is poured out as a sacrifice for you." (Luke 22:19–20)

This verse is speaking about Holy Communion. In the New Testament we find this idea of "remembering" again being attached to both a place (an altar) and a ceremony (partaking of the Holy Communion, one of the sacraments). The fact that this idea is introduced in the Old Testament and then restated in the New Testament should signal to us to the importance of remembering God. In this case, the place dedicated to remembering God is church, which brings me to my next point: we need to go to church, the house for Christians, to remember Christ.

A Word About Remembering

When Christ said, "Do this in remembrance of me" (Luke 22:19), He did not mean the type of remembrance we often think of. For example, if you run into your old childhood friend—oh, let's call her "Yirgedu" (I know . . . a very country name)—at a grocery store, you might say things like "Oh! *Remember* our history teacher?" or "*Remember* the games we used to play?" In this conversation you are catching up with your friend and bringing back events from the good old days. To do this you would have to rely on your brain's ability to recall past events.

When Christ told us to partake in Holy Communion to remember Him, He was not speaking of this type of remembrance. Christ speaks of remembrance that relies on your *faith* rather than your *brain*. That is, Christ's *remembrance* requires you to believe. When partaking in Holy Communion, you are being transported back into time when Christ was crucified. At the particular moment of taking the sacrament of Holy Communion, we are asked to believe that we are witnessing the life of Christ as if we were living with Him two thousand years ago. As a result, we relive the life of Christ and witness His birth all the way to His death. This is what it truly means to remember Christ.

Does God Care If I Go to Church?

Does God care whether you go to church? Really? I think you know the answer already, but since you're reading this, let's take some time to talk about it. Let's begin with a different question: Why did Christ come to this world?

Sure, you're right if you answered "to die for me" or "to give me salvation" or any other similar answers, but this is only half of the correct answer. My brother (or sister or father or mother or auntie or uncle . . . you get the idea), the other half of the answer resides in Christ's love for the Church.

Let me explain. If the *only* reason Christ came to this world was to die and give us salvation, then right after He died on the cross He would have resurrected and that would have been the end of the story. This is not what happened. After His resurrection He stayed in this world another forty days with the disciples. So what was He doing for forty days? He wasn't just hanging out with the disciples—He was instituting a church:

> "Now I say to you that you are Peter (which means 'rock'), and upon this rock I will build my church, and all the powers of hell will not conquer it." (Matthew 16:18)

Christ died for us and the Church!

Christ Died for Us, and . . .

We often, especially in Western society, stress the fact that Christ died for us, but we often neglect to add "and the Church." Following the example of Christ, Saint Paul continued to encourage his readers to go to church. Here is one striking example:

> Do not stop going to church meetings. Some people do stop. But help each other to be strong. You must do it all the more as you see the Great Day coming closer. (Hebrews 10:25–27 WE)

First, to all the skeptics who wondered about whether or not any Bible verses talk about going to church, well, here it is! Second, this verse is as direct as it possibly can be. We can better sense the impact of the verse when we understand its context. The author was writing to a group of Christians who were suffering terribly. They were being persecuted severely, many losing not only their possessions but their lives as well. The writer of Hebrews was telling the congregation to keep going to church no matter what was going on in their lives. This is serious business, friends. I always wonder what this congregation from the first century would say if they could hear the millennials and Generation Z'ers complaining about getting up early one day a week to go to church. Maybe something like this: "You know how many soldiers are trying to kill us just for going to church?

The struggle is real!" And yet they continued going. And we say things like this: "Ya, man—I know. I almost didn't make it out here today because I overslept." But in all seriousness, we have no reason to complain about going to church.

We must understand that Christ died for the Church as much as He died for us. He loves the Church. I get it. Trust me—I do. Going to church is extremely exhausting. Tell me: does this sound familiar? I mean, you have to wake up early to make it to Kidase (liturgy). Once you are there you have to stand the whole time because if you dare sit, you will find angry eyes glaring hard toward you. Then, as if all Ethiopian Orthodox churches have canonized it or something, the AC never works! It is hotter than a blazing summer day. You don't understand anything that is going on, and the service takes forever and ever and ever and ever and ever! But seriously, read these words from Saint Paul:

> So I ask you, brothers, give your bodies to him like a living sacrifice. That is, a holy sacrifice. It will please God. And it is what you should do for him. Do not be like the people of this world, but have a new mind. Then you will prove for yourselves what God wants you to do. That will be good. It will please God. And it will be all right. (Romans 12:1–2 WE)

You see? The very fact that you stand during liturgy, even with your body aching, is part of the sacrifice you are giving to God! Don't think that there is not a good reason for you to go to church! *You* are a sacrifice and a gift for God since He has been kind to you.

Can a Brotha Get Some Sleep?

I know what you are thinking. Maybe you can get on board about the whole going-to-church thing, but you draw the line when someone starts messing with your sleep. I know! I get it! Why do you think Ethiopia is known for its coffee? They need all the caffeine they can get to stay up during a church service! All joking aside, there is a reason for everything within our beautiful Church. Yes, even for waking up early on Sunday mornings.

As I have already stated, the Ethiopian Orthodox Church stands out since it not only preaches about the life of Jesus, but we believe through faith that it is also a place where we can experience all the parts of Jesus's life and be witnesses. This is especially true during the time of liturgy, which takes place early in the morning. For example, if you ever made it on time for Kidase, you may have noticed at the start of Kidase that the deacon goes into the Holy of Holies, accompanied by a priest, and carries something over his head. The deacon starts his journey to the Holy of Holies from a different room named *Bethlehem*, translated as "house of bread." Why? Because the deacon beginning the journey in Bethlehem symbolizes Christ's birth and the city where He was born. Furthermore, their destination, the Holy of Holies, signifies Calvary, the place of His crucifixion. Over his head the deacon carries the holy bread, which will be used as the sacrifice during liturgy. At this moment of the service we believe we are witnessing the birth of Jesus and His journey to Calvary. Through our faith, therefore, we believe we are standing next to our King as if it were two thousand years ago! How beautiful is that?

But why does this have to be so early in the morning? If we

look to the gospel of Luke, following Jesus's crucifixion and burial a group of women discovered the tomb of Christ to be empty (He had been resurrected) "early in the morning."

> On the first day of the week, early in the morning, the women went to the grave. They took with them the things they had made ready. They saw that the stone was rolled away from the grave. So they went in. But they did not see the body of the Lord Jesus. (Luke 24:1–3 WE)

Therefore, we get up early in the morning to relive this event. If we want to relive the life of Christ, keeping it always fresh in our minds, we want to set up the events as closely as possible to the events in the Bible. Imagine that you are directing a movie about Jesus. You would want it to be as believable as possible, right? We want to reproduce the events of the Bible as closely as possible during our liturgy. This way we are not simply preaching the gospel—we are living it!

Ain't Nobody Got Time for This!

Once I heard someone say, "You know you are Orthodox if your church has to do a prayer before a prayer." Funny, right? But nowhere is this truer than in an Ethiopian Orthodox Church. Even a two-syllable word like *amen* can take a good thirty seconds to say during liturgy! This is why it takes all day to get through a prayer that could be said in thirty minutes![2]

It may seem as if liturgy takes forever, but let me ask you

---

[2] Especially the days when the Redskins are playing, you can't help but focus on the time rather than the actual prayer you are participating in.

this: If you had the power to cut out a part of liturgy, which part would you eliminate? The part when we sing like the angels, "Holy, holy, holy is your name"? The part where we ask God to remember those who are sick and poor? Maybe the part where we pray for peace for the whole world? Or maybe the part about God forgiving us? Which would you choose?

Do you see the problem, my friend? If you were able to sit through Kidase, really trying to understand what the prayer was about, you would see why it is virtually impossible to cut out any part of it.

Let me explain it to you this way: One time a great mentor and teacher of mine told me that he had conducted an experiment on a young kid. The kid had been complaining that he found the Orthodox hymns (chants) too boring and found it difficult to connect with them. He just didn't get it. So to put things in perspective, one day my mentor allowed this youngster to listen to any music of his choosing for ten minutes. After the child jammed out to Kanye West, my mentor made him listen to an Orthodox hymn for the next ten minutes. At the end of the twenty minutes my mentor asked the kid which music he liked more. Of course, he affirmed that he liked the music of his choosing more. But then something strange happened: My mentor asked him which genre had actually spoken to his soul. The kid's answer? The Orthodox hymn.

And this, my friend, is the problem. Many forms of music are written to excite our flesh rather than speaking to our soul. When you hear an Orthodox hymn, what is the first thing you want to do? Go to sleep, right? That is because the chants are meant to weaken the body. But it is only when the body is weakened that the soul is strengthened.

Consider the following scripture, which I think really puts this into perspective

> For the flesh desires what is contrary to the Spirit, and the Spirit what is contrary to the flesh. They are in conflict with each other, so that you are not to do whatever you want. (Galatians 5:17 NIV)

I remember when I first started doing Kidase. Honestly, I hated it! I thought it was too long and boring and didn't want anything to do with it. But I also realized that if all these people were coming every Sunday and participating in liturgy, there must be something important in this prayer. So I started to participate in liturgy for only twenty minutes a week. For those minutes I would follow along on my Kidase book (which, if you're interested, you can get on Amazon). I was more interested in what the words were saying than simply chanting along at that moment. But then after a while I noticed something: those twenty minutes turned into thirty minutes, then forty-five minutes, then an hour, and so on until I was able to stand the entire time for Kidase without feeling bored or tired. Just like training our bodies for physical activities as athletes do, we must train our souls for the spiritual realm.

Give it a shot: Start training for your own personal Kidase marathon. Don't worry about other people or what they will say about you. Set up a schedule for yourself. Start out small. Maybe ten minutes if that's all you can do. But for those ten minutes give it your all! Try to follow along the Kidase book and understand what the prayers are saying. The next week try to go at the same time so you can keep doing the same ten-minute section of the Kidase. This way over time you will familiarize yourself with sections of the

Kidase. You can hear parts of it and say, "Ohhh! That's my favorite part!"

The other thing you can do to train for your spiritual marathon is to learn the words! Singing along with everyone else is a lot of fun. It creates a bond among you and other Christians. For example, I remember my college friends would always make fun of me because I never knew the lyrics to any music. Once someone opened a song by Biggie Smalls and everybody started singing along. I was moving my lips, pretending to know the lyrics when I really didn't know the song at all. Even though I felt left out and embarrassed, I learned that participating like this was a lot of fun. If you can follow along and say the chants with everyone, trust me: the time will go by a lot faster and you will be having a good time instead of being embarrassed.

Say Whaaat?

I can't tell you how many times I've heard this: "What are they saying again?" This is the biggest complaint by young folks these days. "I don't understand what they be sayin' though!" And honestly . . . you have a point. The service is not in English, after all. But the question is— What do you do about this?

The key is to seek true worship. True worship *must* be relatable. At the very minimum the worshiper must understand what is being said during the service; this is especially true for the words the worshiper is saying, as he or she should understand those too. This is *exactly* what Saint Paul was talking about when he said this:

> For if I pray in a tongue, my spirit prays, but my mind is unfruitful. So what shall I do? I will

pray with my spirit, but I will also pray with my understanding; I will sing with my spirit, but I will also sing with my understanding. Otherwise when you are praising God in the Spirit, how can someone else, who is now put in the position of an inquirer, say "Amen" to your thanksgiving, since they do not know what you are saying? You are giving thanks well enough, but no one else is edified. (1 Corinthians 14:14–17 NIV)

Yes, this verse is intended to address the issues of speaking in tongues, but speaking in tongues means speaking in a different language. Trust me—this verse is very applicable to us!

Here is good news, my friend! The Church has recognized there is a language problem and is working to mitigate the conundrum. Just in the past few years we have seen a surge in English services, hymns, and sermons. And here you are reading an English book related to the Ethiopian Orthodox Church! There is much more to come— we have only touched the surface. But meanwhile, what more should you do until the worship services are provided entirely in English?

You gotta power through since staying home is just not an option! For example, someone once asked me what my motivation is for serving as I do. I responded by saying, "I do not want the next generation to suffer like I did." What do I mean by that? Especially in my college days, I wanted *sooooooooooooooo* much to get closer to God, but the medium to do that was not available since nearly everything was in Ge'ez or Amharic. Every attempt I made to learn about the Church seemed like such a long and hard journey. Plus, Christianity is already hard enough without adding the extra burden of a language barrier. So I knew I had to power through it.

At least now people have the option of listening to English sermons online and listening to English mezmures. So God has become more accessible through technology. The beautiful thing here is that the Ethiopian community is working on the problems. Hence, we can all work together to ensure that in the future people can worship freely without a barrier of language standing between them and God.

You Mean God Can Hear My Prayers at Home?

Can we get real for a moment? If you have asked this question, why did you ask it? Is it because you wish to pray at home or because you are too lazy to go to church? If we are honest with ourselves, we can see that the true root cause of the question comes from our attitude about going to church to begin with. Either way, we really should talk about prayer for a second.

All my ppls who have asked this question before, listen carefully! YOU SHOULD BE PRAYING AT HOME REGULARLY!

Many who ask this question seem to think praying at home and going to church are mutually exclusive. It is possible, if not necessary, to do both. When we read the Bible we find that there are two types of prayers. The first one is called "solitary prayer." This is the form of prayer we are expected to pray behind closed doors. Even Jesus encourages us to pray at home:

> "When you pray, don't be like the hypocrites

who love to pray publicly on street corners and in the synagogues where everyone can see them. I tell you the truth, that is all the reward they will ever get." (Matthew 6:5)

For this reason you should absolutely be praying on your own at your home.

Communal Prayer

The second form of prayer is communal prayer. You can tell from the word *communal* that this form of prayer is supposed to be done as a *comm*unity. Similarly, Jesus encourages us to participate in this form of prayer.

"I also tell you this: If two of you agree here on earth concerning anything you ask, my Father in heaven will do it for you. For where two or three gather together as my followers I am there among them." (Matthew 18:19–20)

Both forms of prayer are necessary. While solitary prayers are reserved for personalized conversations with God, communal prayers are relevant to the issues of mankind. Solitary prayers may be used to ask God a particular request you may have whereas true worship can be done only in a communal prayer. The bottom line is this: You should be praying at home as well as at church. In this way you can still address your personalized wants in the comfort and privacy of your home while also praying for the problems of mankind through communal prayers when you come to church.

Challenge #1: Purchase an Ethiopian Orthodox Liturgy book. Make sure you have a hard copy so you can take it with you on Sundays and follow along.

Challenge #2: Get an accountability partner. You and your partner should be responsible for reminding and encouraging each other to go to church every Sunday.

Discussion Questions

1. What do you like best about going to church?

2. What are the biggest challenges you encounter while going to church? What can you do to ease some of those challenges?

3. How often do you go to church?

4. What are some common things that prevent you from going to church?

5. Do you regularly partake in Holy Communion? If not, what is preventing you from doing so?

CHAPTER 3

Jesus Is Everywhere!

My beloved brothers and sisters, there are plenty of places where you can hear the Word of God. And absolutely, Jesus is everywhere! Even the Bible teaches that Christ went around preaching the Word of God in people's houses, synagogues, near the rivers, on mountains, and in so many other places. The issue is not about where you can hear the Word of God but about the importance of going to church. As we have been discussing thus far, there are special benefits to going to church. If we reduce going to church to just listening to a sermon, then we miss the complete idea of what going to church means.

Think about this for a second. What is the difference between a regular building and a church? If the only difference is that the church is a place where the Word of God is preached, then does that mean every time you listen to a sermon in your house, your house transforms into a church? Clearly not! There must be other criteria for making a church a "church" instead of a building where the Word of God happens to be preached.

The Bible outlines these criteria when God was talking to Moses as he was getting ready to receive the Ten Commandments. God said to Moses, "Have the people of Israel build me a holy sanctuary so I can live among them. You must build this Tabernacle and its furnishings exactly according to the pattern I will show you" (Exodus 25:8–9).

You see? God is very meticulous when it comes to the place where He ought to be worshiped. In fact, in the next several chapters of Exodus, God instructed Moses about the "patterns" He wanted used to build the sanctuary. Similarly, in the New Testament we see the authority of this pattern recognized:

> They serve in a system of worship that is only a copy, a shadow of the real one in heaven. For when Moses was getting ready to build the Tabernacle, God gave him this warning: "Be sure that you make everything according to the pattern I have shown you here on the mountain." (Hebrews 8:5)

A shadow can only resemble the shape and pattern of the actual being. If this earthly, temporal sanctuary is a shadow of the heavenly, which is eternal, then the patterns of the earthly should mirror that of the heavenly. Furthermore, since the heavenly is not subject to change, the earthly patterns should never change.

Some claim the specificity of the patterns shown to Moses are limited to the Old Testament and since Christ has died for us, the things of the Old Testament are no longer applicable. Surely not all things of the Old Testament are obsolete! For example, was it not in the Old Testament that God instructed people to pray? Are we to say that since prayer was instructed in the Old Testament, we do not need it in the New? No way! In fact, prayer is an eternal concept that does not change. Thus, the patterns of the sanctuary are not meant to change either. Let us examine this for a moment.

To begin, what are the patterns of the heavenly sanctuary? Although the full pattern can be found throughout the Bible, especially in the books of Exodus and Revelation, let us discuss just one of the many instances. God gave Moses specific instructions on how to adorn places of worship:

> "Hang the inner curtain from clasps, and put the Ark of the Covenant in the room behind it. This curtain will separate the Holy Place from the Most Holy Place. Then put the Ark's cover—the place of atonement—on top of the Ark of the Covenant inside the Most Holy Place. Place the table outside the inner curtain on the north side of the Tabernacle, and place the lampstand across the room on the south side." (Exodus 26:33–35)

If you walk into an Ethiopian Orthodox Church today, you will see a replica of the Ark of the Covenant inside the Most Holy Place with an inner curtain separating it from the Holy Place.

The Most Holy Place is divided from the Holy Place by a curtain.

The pattern described above is not temporal. This heavenly pattern was not something God was expecting only Moses to follow but rather all mankind. We should not think of this pattern as an Old Testament concept. We know this pattern was not to be changed because when John received his revelation, he saw the same pattern Moses had seen: "Then, in heaven, the Temple of God was opened and the Ark of his covenant could be seen inside the Temple. Lightning flashed, thunder crashed and roared, and there was an earthquake and a terrible hailstorm" (Revelation 11:19). As you can see, the Ethiopian Orthodox Church truly is a shadow of the heavenly eternal sanctuary.

I Wanna Pray Directly to Jesus!

Every time the topic of intercession—prayer to Saint Mary, angels, and other saints—comes up, people ask this question: Can I pray directly to Jesus? The question stems from the idea that asking for the intercession of saints somehow takes glory away from God.

First, it is important to understand there is nothing we can do to take glory away from God. Second, I am amazed by this question, as there is nothing in the Bible or the Orthodox Church that prevents us from praying directly to Jesus. Really? Who is stopping you? And since we are discussing this now, I will tell you that you *should* be praying directly to Jesus! But let me back up a little bit . . .

What Is Intercession?

You may not be familiar with the idea of intercession. It is act of praying on behalf of someone else. Many describe members of Orthodox Church as not having an intimate relationship with Christ because we often focus "too much" on asking saints to pray on our behalf. This is not the case; in fact, this notion is almost laughable. The Church believes in praying for one another; moreover, the Bible encourages us to pray for one another! Consider the following verses:

> I urge you, first of all, to pray for all people. Ask God to help them; intercede on their behalf, and give thanks for them. Pray this way for kings and all who are in authority so that we can live peaceful and quiet lives marked by godliness and dignity. (1 Timothy 2:1–2)

> And you are helping us by praying for us. Then many people will give thanks because God has graciously answered so many prayers for our safety. (2 Corinthians 1:11)

> Are any of you sick? You should call for the elders of the church to come and pray over you, anointing you with oil in the name of the Lord. (James 5:14)

JESUS IS EVERYWHERE!

Shall I keep going? Okay, maybe just one more:

> "You have heard the law that says, 'Love your neighbor' and hate your enemy. But I say, love your enemies! Pray for those who persecute you!" (Matthew 5:43–44)

Clearly, the Bible encourages us to pray for one another. And if you are honest with yourself, you know you ask everyone around you to pray for you for different things. We do it in a normal conversation. Heck, we even post it on social media!

#prayforme

So where does the idea that it is inappropriate to ask saints to pray for us come from? Why can't we ask saints to pray for us? If it is okay for me to request a prayer, either in my local church or social media or word of mouth, how come I cannot request a prayer (intercession) from one of the saints? In fact, if you think about it, it is *far better* to request a prayer from a saint than anyone else.

Imagine you are going through a stressful period in your life. You are out at the park one day and you bump into two of your friends. Your first friend's name is Pookie. Pookie is known for running the streets. He's a rapper and has been working on his upcoming single titled "Kill'em All." Your boy Pookie can't remember the last time he has stepped foot inside a church.

Your second friend's name is Haile-Michael. Haile-Michael is a deacon at your local church and can often be spotted with a Bible in his hand and a singular scarf (a.k.a. *netela*). The only "single" he concerns himself with is the one Zemari Tewdros will be having out soon. Your old buddy

I NEED ANSWERS

Haile-Michael can't recall when he missed a church service.

Honestly, like really honestly, if you were to ask one of these two friends to pray for you, which one would it be? Obviously Haile-Michael, right? Why? Listen up, home slice: in terms of his relationship with God, Haile-Michael is closer to God than Pookie is.[3]

Haile-Michael   Pookie

Getting Closer to God

The question now is this: Can intercession get us closer to God? I will answer this question with a question: Who is closer to Jesus than the Virgin Mary? She was the mother of God, after all! There is no getting closer to Jesus than this! To digest this idea fully, let's start by taking a look at the events surrounding the birth of Jesus Christ.

---

3 On an unrelated note, if you have a friend named Pookie who is about to get a single named "Kill'em All," you need to find better friends to hang out with.

JESUS IS EVERYWHERE!

Once Saint Gabriel announced to Mary about conceiving Christ, she went to the house of her relative Elizabeth (Luke 1:26–45). Elizabeth, who was also with child, made the following declaration as Mary approached:

> "God has blessed you above all women, and your child is blessed. Why am I so honored, that the mother of my Lord should visit me? When I heard your greeting, the baby in my womb jumped for joy." (Luke 1:42–44)

Ain't that something? Not an everyday occurrence! Yes, mothers can feel their babies moving inside from time to time (or so I have been told), but for a baby to respond by "leaping for joy" upon hearing the voice of the Virgin Mary is incredible to say the least. However, the most extraordinary point for our discussion is the Virgin Mary's response.

> "Oh, how my soul praises the Lord. How my spirit rejoices in God my Savior! For he took notice of his lowly servant girl, and from now on all generations will call me blessed. For the Mighty One is holy, and he has done great things for me." (Luke 1:46–49)

Pay special attention to the phrase "all generations." This is a prophecy for *all generations*. This is not limited to Ethiopians, nor is it limited to Orthodox Christians. This verse includes *everyone!* Yes, even your crazy friend Pookie!

Orthodox Christians do not apologize for recognizing the uniqueness of the Virgin Mary and for continually calling her "blessed." She *is* blessed and holy. Consequently, she is the most befitting person for the position of intercession. Similarly, all the saints and angels are in a better position of intercession than any random Joe from down the street.

Hence, I come back to this question: If we are already asking others to pray for us, why can't we ask saints and angels to pray for us? Especially the ones who have demonstrated a holy and pious lifestyle during their time on this earth?

Some may respond to this question by declaring, "Because they are dead!" People think the dead cannot intercede (pray) for us. They reason the dead cannot hear our prayers. Let's investigate this issue a bit.

Imagine I come to your house for supper (yes, I said supper) and when I leave I forget my phone in your house. You see it sitting there on your coffee table and you say, "Oh, man. It's Dawit's phone! He must have forgotten it when he came over for supper." This statement is revealing and shows us two things: (1) the phone belongs to me, Dawit; (2) the owner of the phone is somewhere else in relation to the phone. Agreed?

Now imagine this! When the day comes for me to depart from this world, there will be a funeral service for me (or so I hope). When my body arrives at the church, you say, "Oh, man. Look! It is Dawit's body!" Once again this shows us two things: (1) the body belongs (or used to belong) to Dawit; (2) the (former) owner of the body (Dawit) is somewhere else in relation to it. Agreed?

So here is the thing: Under no condition when you came to my funeral would you say, "Look—Dawit is here!" Why? Because the essence of who we are is *not* tied up with our bodies. Instead, our essence (our true selves) is part of our souls, which live on! Thus, the dead, whose souls continue to live, can hear our intercession requests. We cannot assume that simply because their bodies are separated from their true selves (that is, their souls) that they somehow stop hearing our requests.

Let's look at a simpler and clearer example in the Bible of a case where we see how the dead continue and hear prayer requests. The example is found in the Gospel of Luke. In the sixteenth chapter Christ Jesus tells a parable about a rich man and a beggar named Lazarus. In the parable we are told that the rich man dies and is taken to Hades. Upon entering, the rich man sees none other than Abraham, who obviously has been dead for thousands of years. The rich man says, "Father Abraham, have some pity!" (Luke 16:24). Here we can clearly see the rich man is making a request to someone who is dead. What's more amazing is that Abraham responds. This signals the notion that dead souls can hear the requests of others! Consider Abraham's response:

> "But Abraham said to him, 'Son, remember that during your lifetime you had everything you wanted, and Lazarus had nothing. So now he is here being comforted, and you are in anguish.'" (Luke 16:25)

From this response we can see that Abraham had full knowledge of the things that had been happening while the rich man was still alive! Once again we see that the dead are fully aware of the events taking place in this world, so they can hear and intercede for us.

What about Angels?

We have seen why the intercession of the Virgin Mary is necessary but what about angels? Angels are seen throughout Scripture, after all. So while we're at it, let me ask you this: What is so special about the angels? Let's start with defining what the word means.

The word *angel* comes from the Greek word ἄγγελος *(aggelos)*, which translates into "messenger." So the angels are messengers of God! Their job is to deliver messages from God to us and take messages back from us to God. We see in the Bible how He repeatedly sends angels to mankind to deliver a particular message. For example, in the case of the Virgin Mary, God sent Saint Gabriel to deliver the message that she would soon become *Theotokos* (the mother of God). God could have delivered the message Himself, but He chose to send the message through the angel. Why?

Angels are sent to us from God to protect us. King David recognizes this deed of the angels in the following scripture:

> He will order his angels to protect you wherever you go. They will hold you up with their hands so you won't even hurt your foot on a stone. (Psalm 91:11–12)

In the book of Daniel we see an example of God using His angels. He sent Gabriel to rescue Shadrach, Meshach, and Abednego from the burning fire (see Daniel 3). There are many instances in the Bible of God sending His messages to man by means of the angels.

But how are *we* to use the angels? This scripture tells us:

> Then another angel with a gold incense burner came and stood at the altar. And a great amount of incense was given to him to mix with the prayers of God's people as an offering on the gold altar before the throne. The smoke of the incense, mixed with the prayers of God's holy people, ascended up to God from the altar where the angel had poured them out. (Revelation 8:3–4)

From this passage we see that the angel was given the task of mixing the prayers of the people of God with the incense. This mixture then ascended to God from the altar where the angel was standing. Thus it is clear that not only is the angel able to deliver our prayers but God allows that to happen! Hence, we should feel comfortable asking the angels (a.k.a. divine messengers) to deliver our prayers to heaven. God created them to deliver messages.

Finally, if you are a left-brained person (you like logic), I have a treat for you! And even if you are a creative right-brained person, I figure the things we talked about in this section can be a bit confusing, so I am including the following chart, which both summarizes and simplifies the main points discussed.

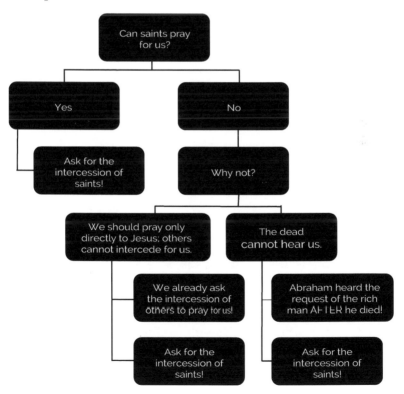

From this chart you can see that there is no real reason to be skeptical of the intercession of saints. If anything, the Bible encourages us to pray for one another. As we discussed, if you are going to ask someone to pray for you, why not the saints? The saints, angels, and the Virgin Mary are all on your side! They are there to support and pray for you so you can achieve your Christian goals in this life. With the myriad of temptations and trials we endure in this world, we should be delighted to have a group of saints to turn to for support. I don't know about you, but I can use all the help I can get.

Challenge #1: Choose a saint of your liking from our Church and learn about his or her life and/or miracles he or she has performed.

Challenge #2: Pray for someone you know who may be going through hard times.

Discussion Questions

1. Describe a time when you needed someone to pray for you.
2. Who is your favorite saint? Why?
3. Do you incorporate intercession of saints into your prayers?
4. What are some of the benefits of asking for the intercession of saints?
5. Why do you think there are many questions surrounding the issue of intercession?

CHAPTER 4

Getting Right with God

Where Do I Begin?

Are you at a point in your life where you feel as though you need more Jesus in you? Don't worry—you are not alone. Everyone reaches this stage of life one way or the other. When we were growing up we were forced to go to church with our parents but did not understand why. However, as we started to grow up many of us began to realize that we must discover God for ourselves and not just for our parents.

This is precisely the stage I was in as I entered my first year of college. Unfortunately, the closest Ethiopian Orthodox Church to Virginia Tech (*Let's go, Hokies!*) was over three hours away, so I found other ways to spend my time. As great as the school was, I realize now that it did not have much to offer other than academics.

Since the town, Blacksburg, is mainly a college town, young people did not have anything better do to than attend "gatherings." (Shhh! That's the code word for *party*, so don't tell your parents!) Although I had grown up in an Ethiopian church all my life, without the weekly church services to keep me on track, I found myself attending more and more of these "gatherings." Without realizing what was happening, I soon found myself consumed in this crazy world of parties and drifting away from God.

Eventually I was so far away from God that I forgot about Him! It came to the point where I couldn't remember the last time I had prayed. In fact, I eventually began to see God more as a burden rather than my Heavenly Father. I wanted to be like every other college student on campus and enjoy myself without any godly restrictions. But at these so-called gatherings, I would always feel guilty for going or doing the things I was doing because I thought I was letting God down. I hated feeling guilty! I wanted to do whatever I wanted and not have to answer to God.

As I continued with my college days, questions related to God started popping into my head. Here is a bullet list of a few:

- How do I know if God really exists?
- Do I even believe in God?
- Does God care if I go to church?

- Out of the many religions in the world, how do I know mine is the right one?
- Why would God create all these sexual desires inside me and order me not to act on them?
- How come God never answers my prayers?
- If God does not exist, am I not wasting my time trying to restrict myself from having fun?

These questions flooded my brain! I could not stop asking them. I finally realized that I had to deal with them. I knew that if I didn't, I would never have a clear conscience and rid myself of this guilt. Here is what I rationalized: If God did not exist, I could finally put this whole "religion" thing behind me and enjoy college life and these "gatherings." On the other hand, if God was real, I knew that meant I had to submit my life to Him and honor Him in every way I could. I decided to spend the next several months doing some deep soul-searching, reading, research, and reflection to seek answers to my important questions. However, before starting this journey, I prayed the following prayer: *God, let me know if You exist! You said to "knock" and You will open the door. Well, I am knocking, so if You don't open the door, it's Your fault!*

This prayer, as bold as it may have been, was exactly what I needed! In the months following the prayer, all my questions were being answered. I treated this quest of finding God like a school project. I started reading books and watching related videos. As for as the existence of God, it came down to one simple "eureka" moment as I was watching a talk by Frank Turek.[4] He was speaking on

---

4 Turek is the author of *I Don't Have Enough Faith to Be an Atheist*, Crossway Books, 2004. I highly recommend this book if you have questions about the existence of God.

the existence of the world and asked the simple question "How did the universe come about?" He went on to explain how everything has to have a cause to come into being. For example, phones by engineers, paintings by painters, and computer codes by programmers. Similarly, the universe had to be created by something or someone. If there was nothing before the universe, that means we are to believe "nothing" created the universe. And that's a bit too silly to believe. Hence, the logical assessment was that the universe itself and everything in it were created by someone—God.

When it came to Christianity, William Lane Craig's explanations answered my questions. He explains this much better than I can in a book entitled *On Guard*.[5] To summarize, he made the case that Christ was an actual historical figure who existed around two thousand years ago, and if we were to study His life, the most reasonable explanation we can give is that Christ is truly the Son of God.

Although I was more certain of the existence of God than anything else in my life, there was something I needed to  do before finishing my journey to find Jesus. I still remember the day as if it were yesterday. In my small college bedroom I got down on my knees and prayed as I had never prayed before: *God, since You have opened the door for me, I am ready to submit my life to You. I will go where You tell me to go and be anything You tell me to be. I will follow You wherever You go.*

---

5 William Lane Craig, *On Guard* (David C. Cook, 2010).

At that moment I felt as if I were being surrounded by all the angels. I could feel Christ holding me! Not only did I believe that God existed, but for the first time I felt His presence! I vowed to walk in the path He would show me and live my life according to His will.

This was it, friends: this was the true beginning of my journey with God.

Don't Focus on Stopping the Bad; Focus on Doing Good

I wish I could tell you I lived a righteous life from that point on and never attended any more "gatherings," but I can't. If my life were a Hollywood movie, perhaps I would tell you that everything was perfect, but it was not. This is real life. Although I had started a new relationship with God, I was still struggling with temptations. Although I had rededicated my life to Christ, I found I was being tested and tempted more than ever!

One of the areas of temptation had to do with the nightlife at college. Every night was the same. We would all gather at someone's apartment and pregame before leaving for a gathering. The shot glasses were up, the music was blasting, and we were fired up. Once we got to the party, we drank some more! I remember going to sleep each night saying, "My body can't take this anymore," but the next weekend I would do the same thing again. I couldn't imagine spending Friday and Saturday nights at home while all my friends were having fun. I just could not stand it. I even talked to my mama about my temptations.

Since we were extremely close, I openly told my mama about the nightlife and the sort of things I did at these gatherings.

Without any judgment, Mama told me to pray once again. This time, however, she told me to say, "God, make me hate this party lifestyle." I thought it was one of the weirdest prayers ever. Who prays before going to a party? Uhm . . . I mean "gathering." This logic did not make any sense to me. But Mama knows best, so I did as she asked. Each Friday and Saturday night before we started . . . well, you know, the things you do on those nights . . . I would go to my bedroom and pray those words. Then, in the words of Kat Williams, I would say, "Tonight we're gonna get messed up!" (I had to clean it up a bit.)

This was an awkward phase for me. I had a little angel whispering to me in one ear and a little devil in the other. Don't get me wrong. I was not completely neglecting God. In fact, all I could do was think about God. I would listen to a sermon every chance I had. I would listen to mezmure everywhere I went. In fact, I loved mezmure so much that I would listen to "ye nishia" mezmure on the way to the gatherings! Seriously, those of you who do not know what that sounds like, get on *YouTube* and type in "ye nishia Ethiopian Orthodox" and check it out. The melody is meant to keep you in a sorrowful state of mind rather than get you fired up for a fun night out at gatherings. So oddly enough, I would go to college parties in this state of mind. I knew deep down I did not want to comply with the college lifestyle. I knew I did not want to be a part of it, yet I just couldn't get out of it. I was trapped. It was too addictive. But I am going to tell you something many people may not say to you. Are you ready?

The Goal of Christianity

The goal of Christianity is not to avoid sin! You can avoid sin all day long, but that still does not mean you have guaranteed your spot in the kingdom of heaven. The real goal of Christianity is to focus on righteous deeds! The heartbeat of Christianity focuses on the fact that mankind is too weak to defeat sin. Consequently, Christ came to die for us because we cannot conquer sin. This is what Paul was talking about when he said this:

> The law of Moses was unable to save us because of the weakness of our sinful nature. So God did what the law could not do. He sent his own Son in a body like the bodies we sinners have. And in that body God declared an end to sin's control over us by giving his Son as a sacrifice for our sins. (Romans 8:3)

So does this mean you have a free ticket to keep on sinning and God will just keep forgiving you? Obviously not! However, the focus should not be on avoiding sin! Instead, we should be striving to do good. The more time we invest in doing good, the farther away we get from evil.

Consider the following example: Should a boy focus on making his girlfriend happy or avoid making her mad? The answer is clear, or at least I hope so. This is simple logic: as long as he focuses on how to make her happy, the less she will become angry. The same way, if you focus on building your relationship with God, you will see your desire for sin beginning to fade away.

This is exactly what was happening to me when I struggled with the college nightlife. As I consistently pushed myself to strengthen my relationship with God, the things I had once found to be entertaining were no longer making me happy. One night at a gathering I remember standing there and thinking, "I could be at home watching an episode of *The Office* right about now." And so I left the scenery and headed home. Suddenly I realized that the prayer my mama had instructed me to pray had worked! I came to hate the college nightlife, and my journey to finding God began.

Your journey may be different, and you must find your own way. Each individual's journey to finding God is unique. What works for one person may not work for the next. However, there is one thing we all must do to begin our journeys: If you are serious about finding God, start with a prayer! Prayer is always the first stop for any journey you are about to begin. Plus, you must be willing to put in the hard work that is needed. Sometimes people expect to build their relationship with God without making any effort, but that is not how it works. You have to do your part. It will take time, so be patient. At the same time, simply allow the Holy Spirit to guide you. If you hold on to Him, He will lead you in the right direction.

I Ain't Kissing Another Man's Hand

I remember once when I took a non-Ethiopian friend to church for one of our Bible study groups. On our way to the class I saw one of the priests, so I gave the traditional bow and lowered my head to kiss the cross he was holding. It was nothing special, just a regular greeting to a priest. My friend, however, was in shock. He asked, "How can you kiss another man's hand?" I suppose that from the angle he was standing at he couldn't see what I was doing and did not realize I was actually kissing the cross the priest was holding in his hand.

Also, this particular priest was my Confession Father. Most of us are accustomed to seeing the priest only when he comes to spray holy water all over our houses. But the priest does so much more! Your priest can also serve as your Confession Father—your friend, counselor, mentor, confidante, and life coach. As your Confession Father, he is invested in your life and gives you the tools you need to help you succeed. You may have a tutor for school or a coach for sports, right? Don't you seek their advice on matters you need counsel on? Why is it any different when it comes to the spiritual world? Thus, the Confession Father serves this purpose. In fact, the Confession Father is not just something I strongly recommended, but it is the will of Christ.

In Matthew 8, we come across the story of man who had leprosy. Although we now know leprosy is a medical condition defined as a skin disease, two thousand years ago people thought those with the condition were being punished by God for their sins. In any case, the leper in Matthew 8 had an opportunity to ask Christ to heal him from the leprosy. Christ healed him, but then something interesting happened.

> Then Jesus said to him, "Don't tell anyone about this. Instead, go to the priest and let him examine you. Take along the offering required in the law of Moses for those who have been healed of leprosy. This will be a public testimony that you have been cleansed." (Matthew 8:4)

Here we have an account of someone going directly to Christ to be healed, yet Christ told him to go to the priest. Similarly, when we sin today, we should go directly to Christ and ask for forgiveness. But this is not enough! Christ wants us to physically go to the priest so he can examine us. The purpose of this examination is much more than simply telling the priest your darkest secrets. As mentioned above, your Confession Father will take the time to understand your story. He will come up with a game plan to help you defeat some of the temptations plaguing you. But more importantly, he will pray for you! And as we have seen previously, the prayer of others (dead or alive) can be extremely helpful!

You Mean I Gotta Tell It All?

The concept of confessing your sins may seem foreign to most of us, but this was actually the custom even in days of the New Testament. Consider the following scripture:

> Such a prayer offered in faith will heal the sick, and the Lord will make you well. And if you have committed any sins, you will be forgiven. Confess your sins to each other and pray for each other so that you may be healed. The earnest prayer of a righteous person has great power and produces wonderful results. (James 5:15–16)

Confession allows you to first admit to yourself that you have a problem. For example, what is the first thing people in an Alcoholics Anonymous meeting say? "I am . . . and I am an alcoholic." Have you ever wondered why they say this? It is because there is a psychological benefit to admitting aloud the problems you have. Furthermore, mentioning sins to other people forces you to be accountable for your actions. As a result, you will have someone to follow up with you and care for you.

In regard to Confession Fathers, Christ gave the priest the authority to forgive sins. Hence, if we don't listen to our priest or Confession Father, we are not fulfilling the wish of Christ. For example, I am a Sunday school teacher. My kids listen to what I say, and they respect me. However, some Sundays I may not be able to attend. On those days I appoint someone else to be in charge of the class. If I learn that my kids were not listening to and obeying the person I put in charge, I see that as disobedience to me rather than to the person I left in charge. The same way, when we don't go to the priests, we dishonor Christ—not the priests.

I've Been Told Not to Take Holy Communion

Has someone told you not to take Holy Communion? No matter who tells you that, do not listen! You need to understand a misconception about Holy Communion. As we already mentioned, Holy Communion is your lifeline! If you feel you have committed sin, then you absolutely need to partake in this holy sacrament. Holy Communion is meant for those who are sick. Trust me, friends—we are all sick. Thus, we all need to take Holy Communion!

Take time to talk to people who partake in Holy Communion and let them tell you how much it has completely transformed their lives! I myself am a testimony. If I go several months without being in communion with Christ, I can feel myself slipping away from Him. You will see an actual difference in your spiritual life when you begin to partake in this sacrament. If you are not sure what you have to do before taking Holy Communion, ask your Confession Father. That is why he is there. He will help you and answer your questions.

Challenge: If you don't have a Confession Father, talk to a priest about the significance of getting one. You don't have to confess or anything; just set up an appointment with him to discuss why it is important to get a Confession

Father. If you already have a Confession Father, your challenge is to introduce your Confession Father to a friend (does not have to be your boo).

Discussion Questions

1. Can you think of a prayer God has answered for you? Describe it.

2. What is the biggest fear you have about confession?

3. What changes do you plan to make in your life to get closer to God?

4. What is the biggest thing preventing you from confessing and/or getting closer to God?

5. Do you know where you can get a Confession Father? Do you need help getting one? If so, I urge you to talk to a priest about taking this step.

CHAPTER 5

Fasting Time . . . Again?

What? You Mean No Chicken?

As we all know, when God created us He made us predisposed to loving chicken. Asking us to give up chicken is like asking our parents not to buy a Toyota Corolla. It is just not realistic! Thus, anyone who has fasted knows the struggle, and it ain't just about the chicken. During fasting, Ethiopians give up other animal products and dairy products. For example, I remember one Wednesday not too long ago I caught a friend of mine eating ice cream. "What are you doing?" I asked. It took him a moment to realize what I meant—it was Wednesday, a fasting day. He contested that he had forgotten and continued to eat the ice cream as fast as he possibly could.

I am sure everyone has a story similar to this about how they "forgot" or simply broke his or her fast under the pressure of some food he or she desired. Let's get real: Have you ever broken your fast when no one was looking? Don't worry. I think everyone has! Fasting is hard, So why do we fast?

Body and Soul

> The flesh desires what is contrary to the Spirit, and the Spirit what is contrary to the flesh.
> (Ephesians 5:17 NIV)

Saint Paul explains here that what the flesh desires the soul detests, and what the soul desires, the flesh detests. Fasting is a time we can give the soul an opportunity to strengthen by weakening the flesh. This concept may seem foreign to some of you, but it is fact! The more time you spend weakening your flesh, the less likely you will be prone to sin and the more likely your relationship with God will strengthen.

You don't believe me? Let's look at an example from the Bible. My main man King David, as pious and holy as he was, had a serious problem when it came to the ladies. We all know the story about Bathsheba and how he slept with her while she was married to another man. Talk about drama! Anyway, it's safe to say that King David, with all his royalty and fame, was kind of a lady's man. But when he was in his old age, his servants decided to provide a young girl to "keep him warm" and to "take care of him" (1 Kings 1:2). Now that's what I call hospitality! Man, oh, man—it was a different time back then. Anyhow, something close to a miracle took place. Consider the following:

> So they searched throughout the land of Israel for a beautiful girl, and they found Abishag from Shunem and brought her to the king. The girl was very beautiful, and she looked after the king and took care of him. But the king had no sexual relations with her. (1 Kings 1:3–4)

What man would be able to sleep next to a beautiful girl, whose job it is to "take care" of him, and have *no* sexual relations with her, especially a man like King David, who had exhibited poor resistance to this temptation? How was it possible for him to do this?

The truth is this: He was old and his flesh was weak. I am sure the desire was there for him to make "happy time," but his flesh would not comply. Therefore, the weaker his flesh got, the less he was able to engage in sin.

Hunger Is a Man's Best Friend

Young folks, listen up! Fasting is your best friend! Resisting sexual temptation is the hardest thing you will ever have to do, but that is the purpose of fasting. It is a tool that will drastically lower the temptation. During fasting you will naturally find yourself gravitating toward the spiritual realm. Even if the thought enters your mind, your body will not be able to comply. Granted, when people have set their mind to sin, they will do so regardless of the situation. However, fasting makes this temptation a lot more manageable.

Once a mentor told me that fasting does the same thing for your body as the brakes do for your car. The purpose of a car is to move from one place to another, but who is willing to get into a car without any brakes? It is not enough to move forward; the car should also be able to stop. If the car is not able to stop it will eventually crash. The same thing is true with our bodies. We need energy to get us through our busy schedules. However, we must learn how to stop or slow down through fasting because if we don't, we too will crash (fall into sin).

Types of Fasting within the Ethiopian Orthodox Church

There are two main types of fasts within our Church. The first type is personal fasting. This form of fasting is either a fast prescribed by your Confession Father or something you decide to do yourself. It can be inspired by a personal trial you are facing or perhaps the need for an extra tool to fight off temptation.

The second type is canonized fasting. Canonized fasting is prescribed by the Church, and followers of the Ethiopian Orthodox Church are expected to participate in it. Canonized fasting can be further broken down into two sub-groups: major fasts and minor fasts. Furthermore, there are seven major canonized fasts. The minor fasts are, for lack of a better term, optional, and we are not expected to observe them. Whether you are fasting the major or minor fasts, it is important to know that each fast has an objective and a theme associated with it. For this reason, before you consider fasting one of them, take time to understand the objective and significance of the fast. Here is a summary of the objectives for the seven major fasts:

The Paramount Fast (ጾመ ገሃድ / *somä gähadə*)

History: As intimidating as the name may be, this is only a one-day fast! The word ገሃድ / *gähadə* comes from the Ge'ez word ገሃደ/*gähadä*, which roughly translates into "to reveal." During this fast we commemorate how God's triune nature was revealed to the world during the baptism of Christ.

Objective: To fast with the hope that Christ is revealed to us today. We ask for a more personal and intimate revelation that can spark a passionate relationship with Him.

Duration: One day during or before Theophany/ *təməkätə* (baptism of Christ) and one day before nativity.

Season: Precedes Theophany/*təməkätə* (baptism of Christ); some also say it precedes nativity.

Fast of Nineveh (የነነዌ ጾም/*yənänäwe somə*)

History: Commemorates Jonah's plea to the people of Nineveh to fast and ask for repentance before God destroyed their land. The people complied and the land was spared.

Objective: This is more of a communal fast wherein we ask God to forgive and have mercy over the world. This fast is perhaps the most applicable today as the world appears to be turning her back on God.

Duration: Three days. Always falls on a Monday and lasts until Wednesday.

Season: Two weeks prior to the Great Lent.

I NEED ANSWERS

Fast of Great Lent (ኣብይ ጾም/ ʾäbyə somə)

History: After being baptized, Christ retreated into the wilderness and prepared for His ministry by fasting. The next three years found Christ teaching, performing miracles, being persecuted, and so much more! At the climax of the gospels, Christ was apprehended and underwent a series of excruciating events that led up to His crucifixion. This period is commemorated during the last week of the fast known as "Passion Week."

Objective: To relive the life of Christ, each week focusing on an event in His life. We recount those events as if they were happening for the first time. The last week, Passion Week, really highlights the passion of Christ. This is the time to contemplate just how much Christ loved us and how thankful we should be for his sacrifice.

Duration: Fifty-five days.

Season: Varies each year but generally begins between February and March.

Fast of the Apostles (ጾመ ሐዋርያት/somä häwarəyatə)

History: After receiving the Holy Spirit but before going into the world to deliver the message of the gospel, the disciples fasted in preparation for their ministry.

Objective: We fast as the apostles did, recognizing our discipleship and responsibility to minister and deliver the same message we have received. Indeed, Christ has risen from the dead!

FASTING TIME ... AGAIN?

Duration: This fast always begins the day after Pentecost and ends on the feast of St. Peter and St. Paul (July 12). But since the day of Pentecost can vary, the duration can be as short as two weeks and as long as six weeks.

Season: Summertime. The timing is probably why many young folks have a hard time fasting this one.

Fast of the Dormition of the Mother of God (ጾመ ፍልሰታ/*somä fələsäta*)[6]

History: The body of the Virgin Mary was assumed into heaven upon her death, and the apostles did not have the opportunity to give her a customary honorary burial. The apostles started this fast to accomplish this delicate task.

Objective: This is perhaps one of the more popular fasts. The fasting period is used to ask for the intercession of the Virgin Mary. Take time to read and understand the prayers offered during this period.

Duration: Two weeks.

Season: August 7–22.

Fast of Advent (ጾመ ነቢያት/*somä näbiyatə*)

History: The Bible tells us that Moses fasted forty days before receiving the Ten Commandments. In addition, many prophets like Isaiah and Daniel fasted in preparation to receiving the Messiah (Christ).

---

6 Don't worry—I also didn't know this was the English name. You learn something new every day. 😊

Objective: With Christmas marking the end of this fast, we fast as the prophets did in preparation for receiving Christ.

Duration: Forty-four or forty-three days.

Season: November 25–January 6 or 7.

Wednesday and Friday Weekly Fasts (ጾመ ድኅነት/*somä dəhənätə*)

History: I am sure most of us know this one. Judas betrayed Christ on a Wednesday by plotting with the people who wanted to crucify Him, and the crucifixion took place on Friday.

Objective: We fast on Wednesday not only to commemorate the betrayal but also to ensure we are not like Judas, "kissing Him" one day and betraying Him the next through our sins. Friday is a day of contemplation and remembering the great passion of Christ.

Duration: Throughout the year, with the exception of fifty days following the resurrection.

Season: Throughout the year.

Can I Call It My Diet Plan?

Can you call it your diet plan? No, man! What are you thinking? Here is the problem. As I said before, the true essence of fasting is starting to be forgotten. For example, have you ever wondered why we are asked to give up breakfast? Most people think it is just to make us feel miserable. But in the old days, during fasting season,

Christians would wake up like every other day and prepare their breakfast. But instead of eating it, they would give their breakfast to the poor who had nothing to eat. If you go to certain monasteries, you will find this custom is still in practice. Before midday you will see a line of homeless people waiting for others to share their morning breakfast with them. Thus, fasting is meant to be a time for sharing.

I often hear people say that fasting is a period when folks should stay away from the "bad things"—a misconception. I have heard of instances where people gave up smoking or cursing or lying during the season of fasting, but being abstinent is not the same as fasting. We abstain because we are Christians. Accordingly, the idea of fasting is to be abstinent of things that are not "bad" in nature and replace them with additional righteous things. For example, when dealing with food, there is nothing wrong with chicken, but we give that up and replace it with spiritual food (prayer).

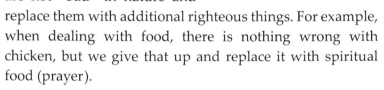

If you are simply giving up things associated with sin, how are you fasting? What have you given up? Whether it is fasting period or not, you should not be engaging in sinful activities. Fasting season is unique because we give up things that are not sinful. *Comprende*?

Finally, fasting is much more than changing the way we eat.

As Saint Yared put it, all our five senses are supposed to be fasting. Hence, our eyes ought to be fasting from watching pointless shows like *Keeping Up with the Kardashians* and focus more on watching a sermon, although some may not consider an episode of *Game of Thrones* to be considered "pointless." Our ears ought to fast from music and listen to mezmure. Our mouths, as we discussed, should be used for speaking to and praising God instead of eating. Our legs should be used to walk to the holy church instead of other places. Our nose . . . you get the idea.

Frequently Asked Questions about Fasting

Question: Are we allowed to eat fish during fasting?

Answer: Different people may give different answers to this question, but the final answer was given by the Holy Synod. They declared we are not allowed to eat fish during fasting. That should settle this debate. However, even if you were not aware of the official ruling, the answer should have been obvious. Think about it. Considering everything we just talked about, if the purpose of fasting is to reduce the amount of food we eat and to weaken our body, then we should gravitate toward the choice that forces us to abstain from fish, thereby reducing the amount of food intake.

Question: What do I do if I'm in college and there is nothing I can eat during fasting time?

Answer: God wants to see how much you have tried. We have just gone over all the ways we can fast. If you honestly have no food choices at the school you go to, talk to your Confession Father to see what choices you can come up with. Whatever you do, don't disregard fasting altogether. You can still pray. You can still fast with your eyes, hands, and legs as we talked about. You can increase the amount of your communication with God. But one thing you should not do is completely disregard fasting just because you are in an area where fasting food is not available.

Question: *If I accidently mess up and eat meat or dairy products, can I keep fasting?*

Answer: The first thing is to continue fasting. Don't let this deter you from the mission you have started. The second thing to do would be to talk to your Confession Father. If you don't have a Confession Father, then find a priest around you and tell him that you accidently ate. If you don't have a priest around you, then pray and ask God for forgiveness and keep fasting! God will understand that you made a mistake. The idea of "I broke my fast so I can't keep going" is a myth.

Question: *If Christ fasted for me, why do I need to? Didn't He die so I wouldn't have to suffer?*

Answer: Christ also slept, ate, and prayed. Christ was an example for the way we are supposed to live our lives. He taught us to pray, how to fast, how to be kind to others, and so on. Just as we don't say we need to stop eating and sleeping (because Christ ate and slept), we also should not say we need to stop fasting because He fasted!

Challenge: You guessed it! Try to do one fast you have not done already. Remember—to get the full effect of the fast, you must learn about the fast and try to fulfill its objectives. If you are already fasting all seven, try to challenge yourself further by giving up something new in the next fast.

Discussion Questions

1. What is the hardest part about fasting?

2. Do you see a change in your spiritual life while you are fasting? If so, what kind of changes have you seen?

3. While you are fasting, other than food, what things do you change in day-to-day activities?

4. Which one of the seven is your favorite fast? Why?

5. Which one of the seven fasts do you struggle with the most? Why?

CHAPTER 6

The Birds and the Bees

Why do I get the feeling that you jumped to this chapter without reading the previous ones? Typical! Well, now that you are here, sit back and hold on tight because we are about to have some fun!

Do I Have to Wait Until Marriage to Have Sex?

Yes. Next question!

Umm . . . You Mean I Really Gotta Wait?

You are not going to let this one go, huh? Okay, well here it goes. Let's talk about the three-lettered word that starts with an "s" and rhymes with "mex." Do you follow? That's right! I said it! S . . . E . . . X!

I NEED ANSWERS

Sometimes adults are nervous about this subject. Talking about sex can be controversial. Thus, as we delve into this discussion, please forget everything you think you know about "the birds and the bees" because I'm going to be as real as I can with you. So the truth of the matter is this: sex is an amazing thing! Everybody should be going out and having sex! It is not just good; it is a gift from God (some may argue it's the best gift He gave us). If you have sexual thoughts, I have good news for you—that means you are healthy! Nothing is wrong with you. Knowing about sex is not the problem. Acting on your thoughts is the real issue. That's right— there is a right way and a wrong way to use sex. If you use it the wrong way, you will get into trouble. If you use it the right way, well . . . it is *amazing*!

The Game of Sex

Sex is like a game. Just like every other game, there are rules you must follow. You can choose not to follow the rules of the game, but the more you break the rules the more the game can mess up. If you break the rules, there are consequences. For example, imagine your main man Pookie and your buddy Haile-Micheal are playing a game of tic-tac-toe. You know how the game works: one person has to use x's while the other is restricted to using only o's. Pookie is using the x's but after Haile-Micheal's turn, he decides he wants to troll a little and starts using o's. This breaks the rules of the game, and the game is over. In the same way, the rules of The Game of Sex (a.k.a. God) has specific instructions on how to play the game. If you do not follow the rules game, the game is over and done and you won't be able to play it. Therefore, I am going to outline the rules for you.

You Cannot Play by Yourself

The first rule is simple and straight forward: you cannot play by yourself! Here is the deal. In the society where we live, masturbation (solo sex) is not condemned. Many even believe it is healthy. Outside the Church, there is almost no social pressure put in place to reduce this behavior because everyone thinks it is acceptable. However, within the Church, masturbation is an extreme embarrassment, and no one even talks about it. The reality is this: within the Church, the temptation to masturbate is an issue of epidemic proportions. Many people, both boys and girls, are struggling with this, and virtually no support group has been put in place to help them overcome this temptation. For this reason, nearly everyone refuses to acknowledge that masturbation is a sin that exists!

I remember once the topic came up in a Sunday school class and the teacher leading the conversation was so embarrassed that he kept referring to masturbation as "this thing" (ይህ ነገር የሚሆነው). He could not even utter the word *masturbation*, which points to a problem of accountability. How are we to hold one another accountable for bad behaviors if we cannot even talk about them? The real tragedy is that since masturbation is committed privately, there is no sense of accountability. Without being held accountable, masturbation can take over your life! This is especially true when pornography is added to the equation.

I NEED ANSWERS

Recent research has shown that pornography has the power to be as addictive as some of the most dangerous drugs out there. I was shocked when I found a study that compared the physical makeup of a drug-addict brain with that of a porn-addict brain. The results were astonishing! The brains looked similar; the porn-addict brain had defects similar to those of a drug-addict brain. This shows that pornography has the same effects as any addictive drug. Dr. Voon, who was part of this study, said, "There are clear differences in brain activity between patients who have compulsive sexual behavior and healthy volunteers. These differences mirror those of drug addicts."[7]

Here is what happens: each time you engage in masturbation—especially with pornography in the picture—you teach your body how to experience the reward of sex without the need of a partner. God intended for the reward of sex to be obtained through a partner.

> To the married I give this command (not I, but the Lord): A wife must not separate from her husband. But if she does, she must remain unmarried or else be reconciled to her husband. And a husband must not divorce his wife. (1 Corinthians 7:10–11 NIV)

When you continue to eliminate the stage where you are intimate with a partner and instead jump straight to the reward, your brain will begin to be rewired to think "no need for a partner." Eventually, when the time comes for

---

[7] University of Cambridge, "Brain activity in sex addiction mirrors that of drug addiction" *ScienceDaily*, July 11, 2014. *Science Daily: www.sciencedaily.com/releases/2014/07/140711153327.htm*. Valerie Voon, et al., "Neural Correlates of Sexual Cue Reactivity in Individuals with and without Compulsive Sexual Behaviours," *PLoS ONE*, vol. 9, no. 7, 2014, doi:10.1371/journal.pone.0102419.

you to have sex with a partner, you will not be able to perform.[8]

This is a new epidemic that many people, especially men, are facing today. Many men in their twenties and thirties cannot perform a sexual act because they have rewired their brain to not experience pleasure from a partner. This is a direct result of watching pornography. How sad! At the same time, this issue impacts women who watch pornography also, as their brains are susceptible to being rewired as well. Pornography in general, because of its extreme addictive nature, is not gender sensitive. When it takes over lives, it does not discriminate.

You Cannot Play with More Than Two Players

This rule is not just about a *ménage à trois*[9] but has more to do with remembering God intends for us to have only one sexual partner. The more we deviate from this idea, the more problems we will encounter. For example, the other day I was watching a TV show about marriage. The show's intent is to counsel couples who are on the edge of divorce and give them the tools they need to deal with their issues. On one episode one of the husbands was trying to convince his wife not to get upset when (not if, but when) he cheats on her in view of the "present day we live in." His logic was

---

8 Brian Park, et al., "Is Internet Pornography Causing Sexual Dysfunctions? A Review with Clinical Reports," *Behavioral Sciences*, vol. 6, no. 3, 2016, 17, doi:10.3390/bs6030017.
9 If you don't know what this means, don't ask.

that the biblical expectation of marriage is unrealistic and that women should be okay with men sleeping (*cheating*) around on their wives! I can't make these things up, people![10]

Sex-onomics: How Did We Get Here?

How did we get here as a society? How did the values of marriage get diminished to this level? One contributor is the way we value sex. We view it as an obligation rather than gift from God. We view it as a commodity. Thus, even my main man Steve Harvey has recognized the diminishing value of sex and encourages his readers to hold on to their "cookie" for thirty days (a term referring to the first time being intimate). His logic is that if a woman gives up the cookie on a first date, then the man will not be motivated to meet her standards and follow her guidelines because he already got what he wanted. Thus, the value of the cookie is cheapened by the fact that it was so easy to attain.

Speaking of cookies,[11] I remember my little nephew once eating a large number of cookies in a short period of time and getting a tummyache. Cookies, as sweet as they may be, if not consumed in the right manner can cause sickness at a later time. There is a biblical story that captures this phenomenon. Let's look at 2 Samuel 13 and read the story of a young man named Amnon.

---

10 Donald L. Hilton, "Pornography Addiction—a Supranormal Stimulus Considered in the Context of Neuroplasticity," *Socioaffective Neuroscience & Psychology*, vol. 3, no. 1, 2013, 20767, doi:10.3402/snp.v3i0.20767.

11 I hope I haven't ruined the edible cookies for y'all.

That Was Cold, Bro

Amnon had a huge crush on a girl named Tamar. He could not stop thinking about her. Because of the cunning advice of his friend, Amnon decided to get her attention. One day he convinced Tamar that he was sick, so she prepared a special meal for him. The innocent and young Tamar took the meal to Amnon's room, whereupon Amnon forced her to have sex with him. As though this were not already evil, the next action of Amnon is horrifying. Consider the following scripture:

> Then Amnon hated her with intense hatred. In fact, he hated her more than he had loved her. Amnon said to her, "Get up and get out!"
>
> "No!" she said to him. "Sending me away would be a greater wrong than what you have already done to me."
>
> But he refused to listen to her. (2 Samuel 13:15–16 NIV)

Seriously? The same guy who couldn't stop talking about Tamar suddenly hated her right after getting what he wanted from her? No doubt Amnon was a jerk! He also represents the mind-set many young men have even today. There is some science behind this.

Before their brains are fully developed, young men are unable to accept all the responsibilities that come along with sex. For example, sex is much more than physical chemistry. Married people know that there is also an emotional component to it. Young men, because they develop at an older age than women, are unable to deliver the emotional part of intimacy. While a young girl desires to be held after intimacy, the young man wants to leave her bedside as quickly as possible. Some research has shown that a prolonged repetition of this cycle for the girl (continued lack of emotional support after sex)[12] causes her to lose interest in sex altogether. This is because the brain, after repeatedly not being able to experience the fullness of intimacy, gets disappointed and has to lower the reward it expects from sex. Eventually, this cycle leads to a complete disinterest in sex. Furthermore, teenagers, especially boys, don't have the maturity level to deal with the responsibility of sex.[13] Their brains are still developing. An adult brain has the ability to manage these feelings in a healthy manner, but young men don't have that capability. This is why a teenage boy will do and say almost anything to a girl to get her into bed. He will even lie. His ability to lie is so sophisticated that he may even convince himself that he is actually in love with the girl.

If we think about it, there are even more pressing issues with having sex before marriage. This act is one of the pillars of marriage that keeps a happy couple, well... happy! Marriage is the time when the man and woman come together under one household and become one in every way possible. But if the couple starts having sex beforehand, or as many couples do today, start living with each other, what is the motivation to get married? This is especially true for the guy if he is

---

12 Amy Muise, Elaine Giang, Emily A. Impett, "Archives of Sexual Behavior," *Post Sex Affectionate Exchanges Promote Sexual and Relationship Satisfaction,* doi:10.1007/10508.1573–2800.

13 Susan M. Hughes and Daniel J. Kruger, "Sex Differences in Post-Coital Behaviors in Long- and Short-Term Mating: An Evolutionary Perspective," *The Journal of Sex Research, 48:5,* 496–505, DOI: 10.1080/00224499.2010.501915 (2011).

getting everything he wants without the need to commit to anything serious. Why would he want to get married?

Every time you engage in premarital sex, you are acting out the motions of marriage. Hence, you will slowly start to see marriage as being pointless. It is like pornography. You will begin to rewire your brain and get this reward of marriage without having to be married.

If couples who live together are practicing marriage, then couples who break up afterward are practicing divorce. Think about it! Without the commitment of marriage in place, there is no incentive to stay behind and work out differences as a married couple should strive to do. Thus, when the shacked-up couple finally gets married (maybe not to each other) and begin to face some problems, the first thing they think about is divorce. Why? Because they have been practicing it for most of their lives. They are pros at divorce because it seems to them like just another form of a breakup. Before you think I am being too extreme, you must admit that the divorce rate in our society being close to fifty percent is extremely alarming.[14] Although there are a number of explanations for this high number, you must admit that the changed attitude in our culture about premarital sex must have played some role in it.

---

14 Andrew J. Cherlin, "Demographic Trends in the United States: A Review of Research in the 2000s," *Journal of Marriage and Family,* vol. 72, no. 3, 2010, pp. 403–419., doi:10.1111/j.1741–3737.2010.00710.x.

Playing the Field: Too Many Players in the Game

In addition to the burdens of premarital sex, when a couple break up and continue the same pattern with multiple sex partners over a period of time, a comparison of the various partners is triggered. For example, each time you get a new phone you observe how different it is from your previous phones. Maybe the screen is bigger or it has better camera resolution or better speaker systems. The same is true each time you get a new partner. Except this time your partner may not be an improvement in all the categories. Maybe he or she doesn't kiss as well as a previous partner. Perhaps the things they say or do during happy times or the steps leading up to intimacy are different.

God did not intend for you to make these comparisons. Ideally, if two virgins meet and get married, they are like a blank piece of paper with no prior knowledge or expectation of sex. Hence, marriage is a platform for them to discover this new world about each other, and they are able to adapt to each other's expectations and wants. On the other hand, people who have had multiple partners have already experienced certain feelings and triggers from their previous relationships. Hence, if their new spouse is not able to deliver, they will be left unsatisfied.

What If I've Already Been Playing the Game and Broken the Rules?

If you find yourself playing the game in the wrong manner, there is still time to fix it! Don't judge me for what I am about to tell you. This happened to me a very, very long time ago. Remember the good old days when cell phones were used to call people? Ya, I am talking about way back then! When I first got my cell phone I was excited, as anyone would have been. So I got my new phone to *actually call* someone, and I accidently dropped it into a glass full of juice I had been drinking. I quickly took the phone out and attempted to dry it. The good news is that the phone was still functioning! However, a small amount of juice managed to get into the screen of the phone, and I could clearly see it at the corner. Now, you promise not to judge me? You have to remember that this was way before smartphone technology was so common, so in my defense, I knew very little about how cellphones worked. Anyhow, every time I looked at my screen, that small amount of juice annoyed me. So I decided to try cleaning it by washing my phone with soap and water . . .

smh

Needless to say, my phone did not work any longer. Case in point: Maybe you made some wrong decisions in the past that caused your "sex game" to malfunction. Stop now! And do not do anything else that can cause it to be further destroyed! You see, had I taken my phone to a repairman right away, there was a real possibility that the phone could have been fixed. But I took matters into my own hands and messed it all up! Similarly, if you believe you have ruined the game, go to someone who can fix it (God). Follow the steps you need to do to fix the game so it can start functioning the right way. If you simply sit and continue to break the rules, however, expect further damage.

You Cannot Play Against the Same Team

Times are changing, no doubt. And as a result, people's attitudes about homosexuality are changing. Nonetheless,

I NEED ANSWERS

God's words are eternal and not up for debate. If you have further questions on this topic, you can skip to the chapter titled "I Was Born This Way," where I deal with this topic in more detail.

How Far Is Too Far?

Now that you understand the game of sex and hopefully have agreed to wait until marriage, you might be wondering how far can you go without crossing the sexual line. Is kissing allowed? What about holding hands? What about...?

The truth is this: chances are, whatever you are planning to do is going too far! Here is the thing about this temptation: It is like a huge magnet that keeps pulling you in. The closer you get to the magnet, the faster and harder you get sucked in. Before you know it, you have crossed the line and committed fornication.

THE BIRDS AND THE BEES

Given the difficulty of trying to resist this temptation, my best advice to you is this: don't play with fire—because eventually you will get burned! If you are old enough to have experienced the temptation, you know it felt almost as if you were being burned alive! You find this intense compulsion to want to do happy time. You feel almost as though you will die unless you go through with the deed. But here is the thing—when this feeling originally develops, if you deal with it in a spiritual manner, it will be a lot easier to manage it. However, if you entertain these evil thoughts, the feeling will continue to spread like wildfire and consume you.

A priest once said that if a girl whose parents are not home calls a boy and invites him over to her house to "study" together, the girl has already committed the sin of fornication. Similarly, if the boy accepts the invitation, the boy does the same. The two meeting up at the house and doing happy time is more of a formality. Think about it—especially when you are dealing with teenage kids. What do you think is going to happen once the boy goes over there? The only thing the two are going to be studying is chemistry![15] Therefore, the plan should be to never allow yourselves to be in this type of a situation. I know it sounds like something your parents may say to you, but I have to say it: if you have not finished school, you should avoid dating in general. However, since that is not always possible, you have to make allowances. Plan to go out in groups, folks. This is true for "studying" too. And please don't stop reading this book . . .

---

15 See what I did there? ☺

The Truth about Relationships

Before you close your mind and turn away, let me ask you a question: When was the last time you saw two teenagers in a relationship that lasted more than three years? You may be able to find one or two examples, but given the number of teenagers starting and stopping relationships, one or two examples is more of an exception than the rule. At this age you think you found the love of your life every other week. That is just the way the teenage mind works. Honestly, it is not your fault. A teenager's body is constantly changing week to week, let alone year to year. This means your mind, along with likes and dislikes, changes with it.

Let's try something here. Let's conduct an experiment. Think back to when you were fourteen. Try to imagine what kind of things you were doing and the things you liked. If you can, try to dig up some old pictures or videos and make notes about how you dressed and acted. If you kept a journal at that age, read it and try to remember what your fourteen-year-old self was thinking about.

After you've done that, think back to when you were sixteen. Do the same thing: Dig through old pictures or videos and take notes about your actions and behaviors. Now compare the two. Do you see a difference? I'll bet you do! The primary difference is probably your physical appearance! I'm sure your looks changed during those two years.

Now let's assume you started dating at fourteen with your dorky smile and dorky attitude. Again, take a look at your fourteen-year-old self and your sixteen-year-old self. If you changed this quickly over a two-year period, so did your "boo." Just in those two years, you both morphed into two totally different people! For this reason, relationships don't tend to last at this age.

You may be thinking, "Who cares if a relationship doesn't last? I'm only having fun!" That might be acceptable for this society, but as Christians we should not think like this.

Dating is the vehicle that ultimately leads to the holy and precious act of matrimony. And as many of you know, holy matrimony is considered one of the holy sacraments offered by the Ethiopian Orthodox Tewahedo Church. This sacrament is considered sacred and precious. Therefore I repeat: Dating is the first step that leads to this holy sacrament!

Dating Is a Spiritual Act

If you are dating there are things you can do to better control sexual temptations. For one, date in public where you will not even have the opportunity to fall. Also, you can talk with each other and agree on a set of boundaries that both of you will not transgress. Make sure to update your Confession Father about your status as a couple (more on this later). Finally, remember that you must pray about this, and do so intensely!

Dating is not meant to be merely a time when two people come together to have fun. Yes, dating can (and should) be fun, but it also needs to have the end goal of marriage. It cracks me up when some people complain about how their partner mentioned the "m" word (marriage) too early in the relationship. That should be on the agenda starting from day one! The primary goal of dating should be to figure out if you are compatible for marriage. In fact, the best pick-up line a boy can use on a girl is this: "Hey—I think I want to marry you. You want to talk about this with me for the next few months?" [16]

The way you decide to talk about marriage is completely up to you. Sure, you can take the girl out to a nice dinner and a movie, but during your conversations you should talk about each other's likes and dislikes. During this time you should be asking yourself this question: Is this person marriage material? If not, you move on!

I know that may sound sudden, but to do otherwise is like driving a car without a destination in mind. Having no goal in mind makes dating pointless. Not to mention, the more you are dating without a purpose, you are allowing yourself to be more prone to sexual temptation. Therefore, use your instincts. If the person you're dating doesn't seem like a good fit, then he or she probably isn't.

How Do I Know If I Have Found My Bae?

One of the questions I am most often asked about relationships is how to know if he or she is the one. The simple answer is this: if you left space for the Holy Spirit between the two of you, and both of you have true love for each other, then you have found the "one." The problem is that many people do not know what true love is about. Let's talk about this for a moment.

What is love? Most of the time people describe love as something you feel. However, love is not a feeling! Love is an action. Love is also a commitment. If we consider the ultimate form of love mankind has ever seen (the love of Christ), we can see real love in action. We know Christ loves

---
16 Guys, feel free to use this one. ☺

us, not because He feels good about us and has butterflies in His stomach but because He died on the cross for us. His death was both an action and a commitment to us. That is love, friends! True love!

Feelings, on the other hand, are variable. They can easily change. Think about it. You can be happy in the morning and angry at lunchtime and happy again by dinnertime. If you think love is a feeling, you are in trouble, my friend. Just as you are feeling good about your partner now, you are going to find yourself feeling bad about him or her soon enough. If it is true love though, "in sickness and in health," as they say, you will not leave your partner's side. The reason these vows are exchanged on the wedding day is to remind the groom and bride that their feelings toward each other may change, but their commitment will remain!

If love is a commitment, you need to ask yourself if you can handle all the negative traits and weaknesses of your partner. Although it is important to think about all the positive traits of your future hubby or wifey, take time to learn about his or her weaknesses as well. Once you discover the darkest side of the person, ask yourself this: Can I put up with this forever? If you can honestly say that you are willing to put up and deal with this trait, which may never change, then you have found the one! Oh, and that's the other thing. Don't expect the other person to change, so be realistic about this.

As for being realistic, also keep in mind that there is no such thing as the perfect partner. People spend too much time using unrealistic standards as they look for a person. The perfect way to see whether your standards are unrealistic is to ask yourself if you meet the same standards you have set for your significant other. In other words, you are not perfect, so don't expect to find a perfect person.

On the other hand, if you are constantly finding yourself in a negative relationship and attracting all the wrong people, ask yourself why this is happening. If you are in this kind of negative cycle, it is time to reflect on your life and ask why you are attracting all these unsuitable people. You may want to stop looking for your future baby daddy at the club while getting turnt up to, "Gurl, you look good—won't you back that thang up?" Seriously, is that how you want to start your journey into marriage?

Once you get to know the person you're dating, it is always advisable to introduce him or her to your Confession Father. That can save your relationship in ways you cannot imagine. This is especially true for younger dating couples since the Confession Father serves as a mediator and counselor for both. He has no special interest, unlike family who clearly will side with their own relative. The only wish of the Confession Father is to bring both of you closer. If your partner refuses to meet with your Confession Father, you may want to hold off on the wedding. Think about it. If you consider yourself to be in a serious relationship and your partner refuses to meet your mamma, what would you think? That means your partner is not taking the relationship as seriously as you are. Also, if your partner is not Orthodox, he or she should be respectful and willing to meet all the people who play a big role in your life. So either way, be sure to bring your Confession Father into the mix.

After the dating period, if the time comes when he pops the big question and she says yes, you are ready for the wedding! Congratulations! It was God who brought you to this stage, so don't forget about Him now! Thank Him! Praise Him! Remember: God created marriage as a gift for mankind. And remember that with Christ's protection, man and wife are able start their life together knowing they will be protected from all evil.

> "'This explains why a man leaves his father and mother and is joined to his wife, and the two are united into one.' Since they are no longer two but one, let no one split apart what God has joined together." (Mark 10:7–9)

Challenge for Men: Step 1—Read the book of Proverbs in its entirety. Step 2—Highlight all the advice King Solomon gives about women. Step 3—From the points he made, identify which ones you have followed and which ones you have not.

Challenge for Women: Step 1—Read and memorize Proverbs 31:10–31. Step 2—Identify which aspects of your life differ from those of a virtuous woman.

Discussion Questions

1. Why is it difficult to play the game according to the rules of God?

2. How can I protect myself so I do not break the game?

3. What things should I look for in a girl/boy when I start dating?

4. What are some issues I should expect when I am dating?

5. How do I know if I am ready for marriage?

CHAPTER 7

I Was Born This Way

God created Adam and Eve, not Adam and Steve (insert laugh). Have you heard this quasi-funny joke when referring to homosexuality? Don't worry. I promise there won't be any in this chapter. I also promise not to go off on a rant about how God burned all the gay people in Sodom and Gomorrah and that it's the same fate that awaits you if you live that lifestyle. Oh, man—that sounds harsh . . .

The purpose of this chapter is to address questions raised by someone who may identify as part of the LGBTQ (and any other letter that may have been added since) community. If you identify as such, I ask you to read this chapter with an open mind. No one is going to force you to change your mind at the end. All you have to do is read.☺

Doesn't God Love Gay People?

♪What's love got to do, got to do with it.[17]♪

Sorry! I had this song stuck in my head. I just had to let it out because love has plenty to do with this topic. (Thanks, Tina Turner.) The answer to the question is this: Yes! God loves gay people. I must admit I am bit perplexed. On one hand, I can't believe someone would even ask this question since God loves what He has created unconditionally. On the other hand, given the culture we live in, I can see why someone may ask.

Some people are guilty of hiding behind Scripture, trying to justify their homophobic tendencies. This is a serious, deep problem in the Christian community and even much more in the Ethiopian-Christian community. Someone once told me they threw away their schoolbook after one of their gay classmates picked it up by accident. When I pressed for an explanation for this rather bizarre behavior, I was bombarded with Bible verses about how homosexuality is a sin. The problem is that there is a big leap between homosexuality in the Bible and throwing your book away because someone you don't like touched it. By referencing the Bible, however, this person was able to escape real responsibility for his actions. The truth of the matter remains: this behavior is homophobic. There is no scripture one can quote to justify this action. Nonetheless, some people do rationalize homophobic tendencies by hiding behind scripture.

The Bible tells us that "God so loved the world that he gave his one and only Son, that whoever believes in him

---

[17] Terry Britten and Graham Lyle, "What's Love Got to Do with It" (Capitol, 1984).

shall not perish but have eternal life" (John 3:16 NIV). My friend, this verse is as relevant to you as it is to me! You must know that Christ came and died for you! He loves you very much! You are a child of God, and no one can ever take that away from you!

Let's get real for a moment. Even though God loves you, other people may not. Even here in America we have seen young gay children being bullied and tormented for identifying as homosexual. This phenomenon is exacerbated within the Ethiopian community. If you have been a victim of such hate crimes, I am sorry you had to endure that. No one deserves to be treated in this fashion. You, like everyone else in this world, deserve to be treated with respect and honor. Remember: you have Christ on your side and nothing can destroy you. I urge you to simply focus your eyes on Christ and ignore the noise around you.

I Am Who I Am—I Can't Help It

Focusing on Christ means you must be accountable for all that Jesus taught us. We cannot pick and choose which lessons to follow. Thus, we Christians must be willing to at least attempt to live our lives according to His teachings. With that being said, let's go ahead and tackle one of the most debated questions: Are people born gay or do they choose to be gay?

This question is significant, and I hope you can see why. If you are born gay, that means God created you to be gay. Hence, homosexuality cannot be a sin. How can something God created be a sin? On the other hand, if you choose to be gay, then you can choose to be un-gay and stop sinning. Therefore, the real question is this: What would it mean to be born gay?

Have you ever seen a gay baby? Do they have a natural tendency to gravitate toward a pink baby-bottle over a blue one? Do they have a distinct gay cry that can be easily identified? Do they have a better fashion sense at six-months than their straight counterparts? Obviously not! Thus, you were not born gay just as I was not born straight. When we were babies, you and I didn't have time to tackle big issues like homosexuality. We had a pretty hefty schedule with all the pooping, crying, eating, and sleeping. So, that can't be it . . .

Does this mean you choose to be gay? Really? I mean, who would choose to be estranged from their family, church, community, and everything they ever wanted? This is the reality of many people once they come out of the closet, as many in the LGBTQ community are the targets of hate crimes. No one chooses to endure all that negativity. Hence, no one chooses to be gay.

So if you are not born gay or choose to be so, what is going on? The desires and feelings associated with homosexuality are not chosen. That is to say, a person's homosexual feelings do not result from his or her own choosing. Moreover, this does not mean you were born gay. So if you are not gay from inception, by the very definition other factors have influenced your desires and are affecting you. After all, this is the whole nature-versus-nurture debate. If you were not born gay, nurture (your environment) has influenced you. I am not suggesting that there are specific elements in the environment to cause a person to be gay, but I am suggesting for reasons not known that your environment does influence many aspects of your perspectives. Sexual desires are not exempt from this.

There Is Something Wrong with You!

I remember watching a debate between a pastor and a member of the LGBTQ community about gay marriage. The pastor said something like this: "If you come to Christ, He can remove this sin from your heart." In rebuttal, the person from the LGBTQ community said, "There is nothing wrong with me. I don't need to be fixed."

This statement shows a serious flaw in understanding of Christianity. The reason Christ came to this world and died for us is because there is something wrong with *all* of us! Think about it—it is not just an LGBTQ issue if we think we are not all broken. Once you begin to think there is "nothing wrong with you," you lose the desire to seek Christ as your Savior. This is, after all, what Christianity is about! We are to seek Christ with all our might, believing that we need to be healed from this cancer we call sin.

If you read the previous chapter, you will recall that the goal of all Christians should be getting close to Christ rather than avoiding sin. The same is true here. Approach God with all your might and surrender every part of your life to Him. That should be your priority—not putting an end to being gay! You can be straight as an arrow, but if you have no relationship with God, your spiritual life will still be in trouble. Hence, the objective is to journey toward Christ, surrendering yourself to Him. Once you do so, you must allow the Holy Spirit to guide you to the truth.

Is Homosexuality Really a Sin?

Before we answer this question, let's talk about the Bible for a second. The Bible is meant to be used like a mirror. You stand before a mirror to see if you have imperfections you can fix. If you see something on the mirror that you don't like, you can't get angry at the mirror! The mirror is not lying, and it is not broken. The imperfections are yours, and you have to fix them. If you cannot, try going to someone who can. If he or she cannot fix them, you must learn how to deal with the imperfections. We all have them, after all. Lord knows, each day I stand before the mirror and witness my rapidly receding hairline. There is nothing I can do to the mirror. I have to accept the reality and move on. Thus, regardless of what you see, you must understand that the job of the mirror is to point out things to you.

The job of the Bible is to point things out to you as well, particularly your imperfections. When we look to the Bible, we may not love everything we see; in fact, some things may even offend us. Nonetheless, we cannot get angry at the Bible. And we certainly cannot attempt to correct the Bible. It is not broken. The Bible is there to correct us—not the other way around.

Now that we can conceive of the Bible as a mirror, we can see what it says about homosexuality. Unmistakably, the Bible says it is a sin. There are no *ifs, buts,* or *howevers* about it. It is as clear as day. Some people suggest that homosexuality is found mainly in the Old Testament, where it also tells us not to eat pork and whatnot. These arguments are extremely misleading since the way the subject of homosexuality is discussed in the Bible is unique.

Then and Now: The Cultural Argument

Consider the following two statements: "Do not spit on someone's face" and "Do not drink and drive." Both these statements are statements of command; however, they do not hold equal weight. Given the current society we live in, spitting on someone's face is considered to be rude and disrespectful. Therefore, the commandment not to spit on someone's face is a social guideline for how we ought to live in this present society. However, if you go to the countryside of Ethiopia, you will learn that elderly people spit on the face of young people as a sign of respect! I myself have been "honored" to witness this rather unusual cultural trait. I remember one time an elderly lady decided to bless me by spitting all over my face. For her she was doing something very nice for me. I, on the other hand, would have been okay with not receiving this particular blessing.

The statement "Do not drink and drive," however, it is much more than just a social guideline. It a law that each person is expected to honor. If you witness someone drunk while stumbling over to his or her car with the intention of driving it, I trust you would interfere and take the person's keys away. Why? Because the statement about not being a drunk driver is not a cultural-dependent statement but rather a statement that remains to true regardless of the time or culture we live in. So while both statements are commandments, we do not deal with them in a similar manner. In the same way, when reading the Bible we should discern statements about what type of food we ought to eat differently than statements about homosexuality. When it comes to homosexuality, the Bible makes it clear that it was a sin then, it is a sin now, and it will continue to be a sin in the future regardless of the culture or society we live in.

The Context Argument

Some argue that the Bible is over two thousand years old and cannot be read in the lens of the twenty-first century. Although there is some truth in this statement, the Word of God is eternal. Therefore, the things it says that were true two thousand years ago are true today. Again, we cannot pick and choose which sections of the Bible we want to believe. It is not a "print on demand" kind of thing. Those who argue the Bible is outdated are actually doing so because they feel the Bible is preventing them from doing something their flesh desires. Remember—the Bible is our mirror, and we may not like what we see. However, we have to accept what it says and be willing to fix our imperfections. This is true for everyone, gay or straight.

The Semantics Argument

A few even argue the Bible never used the term *homosexuality*—therefore, homosexuality was never condemned. This is again an attempt to misdirect the teaching. The word *homosexuality* does not appear directly in the Bible[18] because it was not a term made available at the

---

[18] The Oxford Dictionary places the origin of the word *homosexual* to be in the late nineteenth century.

time it was being written, but we all know what Paul meant when he wrote this:

> Because of this, God gave them over to shameful lusts. Even their women exchanged natural sexual relations for unnatural ones. In the same way the men also abandoned natural relations with women and were inflamed with lust for one another. Men committed shameful acts with other men, and received in themselves the due penalty for their error. (Romans 1:26–27 NIV)

I could continue listing verse after verse about how the Bible openly condemns homosexuality, but I think that is pointless. The focus should be not on homosexuality but on Christ! With all your might, your primary goal should to build an intimate and close relationship with Him. Approach Him and allow Him to guide you.

"You Can't Pray the Gay Away"

Have you heard this before? "You can't pray the gay away." This is a slogan used by gay activists to criticize the Christian community about their approach toward homosexuality. They argue that since homosexuality is not something that can be changed, you can't simply pray about it. Furthermore, they don't think prayer will change anything. Once again, this speaks volumes to their misunderstanding about prayer. What happened to faith, my friends? What happened to trusting the power of prayer? Do not forget John's words:

"This is the confidence we have in approaching God: that if we ask anything according to his will, he hears us" (1 John 5:14 NIV). And don't forget these words of God:

> "If my people, who are called by my name, will humble themselves and pray and seek my face and turn from their wicked ways, then I will hear from heaven, and I will forgive their sin and will heal their land." (2 Chronicles 7:14 NIV)

My dearest brothers and sisters, questioning the power of prayer is questioning the strength of God Himself. We must believe God has the power to enable us to do anything! If you hold on to Him, you will find that God will guide you. Keep praying and keeping getting close to God. Face your weakness in truth. Use your Bible as your mirror and understand that God has a big plan for you and loves you very much. Do not turn your back on Him. Also, know that He is your Savior. This means you have to be willing to admit you are sick and infested by sin. Thus, only when you are willing to admit this problem and receive Him as Lord and Savior can you begin to get healing.

Challenge: Make Psalm 23 and 51 part of your daily prayer.

Discussion Questions

1. Do you think homosexuality is a sin? Why or why not?

2. What recent changes have you seen at school or work involving the LGBTQ community?

3. Do you think the Church's position about homosexuality is driving people away from the Church? What solution would you suggest?

4. As Christians, how should we approach someone from the LGBTQ community?

5. What advice would you give someone who identifies with both the Ethiopian Orthodox Tewhaedo Church and the LGBTQ community?

CHAPTER 8

The Struggle Is Real

Dealing with Mental Illness

Initially I did not plan to include this chapter in this book. However, I have seen over the years more and more people affected with mental illness and thought it would be a good idea to do so. Let me start by saying that I am not a psychiatrist or medical professional, but I do have some experience in dealing with mental illness and thought it would be good to share my personal story. Please—if you know someone (including yourself) currently experiencing depression or any other form of mental illness, speak with a doctor as soon as you can. Finally, even though I may not be able to provide any medical advice, I believe that by speaking about this topic we can get rid of the stigma behind mental illness and encourage more people to seek help. I hope other people can relate with my story and learn from it as well. So here we go!

I NEED ANSWERS

"I'm Not Gonna Take Him—You Take Him!"

Have you seen movies that show kids arguing over whose team the last kid to be chosen will be on? The kids begin to chant, "You take him!" and "No! You take him!" Well, this was my reality almost on a weekly basis in elementary and middle school. Before you smile, thinking this event was funny, understand that comments like these caused me to hate my upbringing.

I hated going to school! For one, I went to a predominantly white school. I could barely find kids who even looked like me. I remember random kids would come and touch my hair and say things like "How do you get it so nappy?" To make matters worse, I had just come to the United States. I had an accent, and others made fun of my English. I was also born with a leg problem that caused me to limp whenever I ran.

All these things created the perfect storm to make me the victim of severe bullying. Especially in elementary school I had no friends and spent most of recess period talking with the custodians in the cafeteria instead of playing with other students. At the peak of the bullying period, one of the popular kids came up to me and patted me on the back, telling me he thought I was a good friend and to always keep my head high. Unbeknownst to me, the kid had tapped a note behind my back that read, "Kick me." I was humiliated. I remember how awful I felt. Another time one of my classmates wrote a love letter, forged my signature on it, and gave it to another boy! Everyone made fun of me for months. I felt it would never get better. I hated the students! I hated the school! I hated my life!

The beacon of hope I had at that time was the Sunday school

program at my local church. My school week was lonely, and I used to count down to Sundays. I wish I could say I looked forward to learning about God and getting close to Him, but the reality was that I had some great friends at Sunday school. Actually these were my only friends! Sundays were not only an opportunity to escape the world of bullying but also a time when I was surrounded by people I knew loved and cared about me. At church I was able to make lifelong friends at a young age, many of whom I am still in contact with to this day. I am grateful for them.

My Life Got Better

I was so glad when my parents bought a house in another part of town, which meant I would change schools. Usually kids are disappointed to learn they are moving to a new school, but not me! I felt this was the greatest gift my parents could have given me! The new school was a lot more integrated then the previous one, so I didn't have to look far for folks who looked like me. I could identify with many of the other students. For the first time in my life I was able to find people to sit next to in the cafeteria! I befriended several of my classmates, and the bullying days felt like a thing of the past.

Bullying Is Real and So Is Depression

Although things went really well at my new school, I decided to let my parents know how much I had been battling with depression—especially in the earlier part of my childhood. I told them about the bullying, but they never really understood how badly this had impacted me. Although I was no longer being bullied, I thought they needed to know just how bad it had been. At the end of my high school career I decided to write them an email explaining how severe the bullying had been and just how much I had hated my life during those years. In the email I went on to explain how I had even had suicidal thoughts.

My parents, as loving and caring as they are, still did not understand. They just didn't get it. I think this is true of many Ethiopian parents when it comes to issues like bullying, depression, and mental illness. Bullying is a serious epidemic in our society. Many children become victims and suffer a great deal of depression because of it. When it comes to our parents, and I say this with love, they don't seem to understand the concept because most of them grew up at a time where they were faced with serious issues like the Ethiopian Red Terror, and most of them witnessed many of their friends dying and being tortured. In contrast, the idea of a child in America complaining about other kids making fun of him simply does not seem all that serious for them. For the American children, however, their only frame of reference is their reality in this present society. Bullying, with no prior reference to other hardships, can feel as traumatic as any events our parents had to deal with.

Our parents don't seem to know how to handle these issues, but this is not their fault. They grew up in a very different time and under different conditions than we did. We can't blame them for not understanding because at the end of the day depression is depression— whether it is caused by something that seems small or big is irrelevant. Once people are depressed, they are depressed.

If you are battling with depression, understand that you are not alone. If you have been getting bullied at school, try talking to someone who will listen. If you feel as if your parents do not understand, talk to a guidance counselor.

Counseling can be more helpful than you may think. Tell someone you trust.

I Can Fly

My big turnaround came when I heard a speech given by Dr. Nikki Giovanni, a poet, writer, and educator. I remember it as if it were yesterday. I had just been accepted to Virginia Tech, and the school had prepared a "Welcome, Incoming Freshmen" sort of event. Dr. Giovanni was invited to give a talk. Her speech was about the importance of finding a purpose for your life. She challenged us to ask ourselves why we were brought into this universe and what contributions we can make to it. Put simply, I was captivated, as I hadn't really thought about things like this before—not this way—so I began to wonder about the purpose of my life.

I sought the answer to this question for several years. I experimented with different ideas ranging from tackling poverty to collecting books for kids in Ethiopia. I even cofounded a nonprofit named "Children of Ethiopia Organization" (C.E.O.). Eventually I realized that my purpose revolved around church services, so I began to serve the Church almost every day! I decided to dedicate all my time to church. For the first time I felt my life had value. I knew I was created for a reason. Life had a new meaning behind it. I was excited to wake up in the morning because I knew God had a goal and a purpose for me.

For me the best remedy I found for depression was understanding what my purpose in life was. I advise you to do the same whether or not you are dealing with depression. Your entire life will completely transform once you know why God created you. You will have a reason to wake up in the morning. Especially when you are enduring hardship, you will find the strength to keep pushing forward because you will know you are in this world for a purpose. And you are! Your life has value. You matter to your parents, friends, and community. Most of all, you matter to God!

Is It All Over?

Once I found my purpose, nothing was more important to me than serving God. I felt as though He had saved my life! I had been a nobody, feeling depressed and sad. Now that I knew God, I was happy and had a purpose for my life. I owed Him everything! All I could think about was how I could continue serving Him. Thus, I continued teaching in my church's Sunday school program as much as I could until I graduated from college. When I came home for the holidays, I never missed church on Sundays. Even when I went away to school, I would follow up with my students, calling them sporadically and checking up on them. I also spent the time away preparing lesson plans for the students.

When I graduated from college I landed a promising job working for the government. I had a decent amount of money that allowed me to purchase a house when I was only twenty-five. I am not writing this to boast about my life but to boast about the amazing work God has done in my life. Yes, I was thankful for the fruits of my labor in the government job, yet no matter how hard I worked, something was off. I was not fulfilled: the money, job, house—all of it—were not bringing me any happiness.

I knew where my happiness came from, and that was from God. So after much deliberation, I decided to give it all up and head to Ethiopia to live in a monastery. I figured that by fully immersing myself in a holy environment I could finally fulfill my purpose of ministering the Word of God. I spent over two years praying and planning out this mission in detail. Before my departure date to Ethiopia, however, I started having severe leg pains. This was not anything unusual given my long history of leg problems. By this time I had undergone two leg surgeries in an attempt to correct my condition. These recent pains were chronic; therefore, a long-term remedy was in order, especially since I was about to travel to a remote, secluded part of the world where I may not get medical treatment. After seeing several doctors, I eventually found myself consulting a neurologist about my condition. After preliminary testing, I was advised to get an MRI scan. The results were not what I expected. They found a lesion on the left side of my brain.

Upon hearing the news, I felt sick to my stomach. I was left with questions; I felt isolated and defeated. How could God allow this to happen? I was getting ready to surrender all parts of my life to Him, but instead He was . . . I didn't know what He was doing. I was angry, upset, confused, and scared. I honestly did not know what my future would look like. I did not know if this was an issue that would progressively worsen. I did not know if would cause my death. I was empty and I was anxious. I could not sleep. Thus, I once again trembled back into the world of depression.

Once you are stuck in this world it is very hard to be optimistic. The only thing you can see are the negative outcomes. Nevertheless, I decided to tell my close friends about what I was going through. Sharing with them allowed me to get rid of some of the burden. I suddenly felt that I was not left alone to deal with this on my own. I now had a support group. My friends were constantly praying for me and checking up on me. This gave me hope. Their encouraging words helped me stay focused and not give up on the grace of God.

I remember on a Friday afternoon, which happened to be a Good Friday, one of the doctors called me to let me know that the lesion was caused by what he called an *"in utero* stroke." This means that I had experienced a stroke before I was even born! The good news was that this was a one-time impact and the lesion was not expected to worsen. Thank God! The doctor told me I should consider myself to be fortunate and informed me that other patients with similar diagnoses are left with much more negative outcomes.

Do Not Go Alone

The scare of losing your health can be overwhelming, yet even worse is experiencing death in the family. No one can say anything to make that deep pain in your heart go away. The naturally tendency is to push everyone away and try to deal with your emotions by yourself. As painful as it might be, being by yourself and dealing with heavy unfortunate circumstances will not ease your pain.

Obviously the first thing you want to do is pray. Events such as this can cause you to be angry at God, and that is okay. If you are angry . . . tell Him! *Let him know how angry you are! Scream at him! Yell at him!* God is a great being. He can handle it. He would rather you scream and yell at Him than to stop speaking with Him. And as painful as the moment may be, the only being who can truly help you heal is God. Don't forsake Him.

Whatever you are dealing with, after prayer speak to someone. For me I have been blessed beyond measure! I have an amazing father and mother who are completely supportive. Even when I ignore them and act as if I don't want to talk to them, they are constantly checking up on me to make sure I am all right. I feel safe and confident talking to them about anything. The same is true with my older brother. He is there to give that elderly advice (don't tell him I said that) and provide any support I need. I suggest you do the same. Talk to your family members—particularly when you are going through hardships such as a death in the family. Your family can be extremely thoughtful and understanding if you give them the chance.

Last, talk to friends you can trust. I can honestly say I have the best friends in the world. They are more like family than friends. They have been there for me through the good and the bad. Get yourself a set of friends like these. You don't have to announce your problem to the world but let someone you trust know what you are going through. If nothing else, they can listen! Sometimes that is all we need—someone who will listen to us.

Claustrophobic, Anyone?

Having cleared the medical issues, I headed to Ethiopia to finally pursue my dreams of serving God. I went to a monastery named Debre Libanos. For those of you who have never been, I strongly suggest you visit one day when time permits. Staying there was truly a blessing. I was able to connect with God and learn about the Church. I felt reassured that this was exactly where I needed to be.

My experiences in Ethiopia were not without challenges, however. There was a constant shortage of water, power was more of a luxury then a necessity, and several days I ate nothing but *kolo*. Plus, there were bed bugs[19] everywhere. Then there was the time I was chased by a wild dog at two o'clock in the morning (long story). But none of this equaled the hardship of being lonely.

My room was just big enough to hold my bed and some of my luggage. In fact, the room was so small that the door would not open all the way. On average I spent eighteen to twenty hours a day in that room. I left my room only to go to the bathroom, to go to church in the morning, and to go to class. That was it! I had very little interaction with other people in the monastery. For the year and a half I spent in the monastery, I was in that room praying or studying. Thus, there were nights where I felt extremely lonely. Sometimes I would talk to myself until morning. I would tell myself jokes and attempt to entertain myself. The point is, being alone is not fun at all.

Feeling lonely is another reason many people find themselves falling into depression. Human beings are meant to interact with others. If this desire is not met, then loneliness follows. Even if they don't sink into depression, people often find themselves trying to fill in this void by staying busy with other activities. This is good as long as the activities are good ones. However, some turn to alcohol or drugs to fill the void of loneliness; others might constantly find themselves in an unhealthy relationship.

If you believe in God, you know you are never really alone. You may lack human companionship; those "around" you may seem like they are not "around," but God will never leave your side. I promise.

---

19 Oh, the bed bugs . . . sorry . . . this is bringing back some memories!

I'm not debating the issue. Being lonely sucks! To borrow a line from my favorite TV show, *Recess*, this whomps! If you are feeling lonely, leave the house. Do something. I find that going to the gym allows me to release some tension I may be feeling. It relaxes me. Go to the park and walk around. Keep yourself busy in a good way that is not destructive or harmful. Plus, I bet if you look hard enough, you will find healthy, God-loving people like you to spend time with. Pray for this, and God will lead you to one another!

It Wasn't All Bad

The struggles in life are real, my friends. We each have our own. I don't want to seem like an ungrateful brat. Truth is, my life is pretty awesome. Yes, I endured some setbacks, but who hasn't? That is life. I have a great family, friends, and most of all I have a great God who loves me. I can't complain. I choose to highlight the negative side of my life because it is these struggles that mold us into better versions of ourselves! It is in these situations we naturally gravitate toward God. The more we rely on God's strength instead of ours, the more we are able to endure bigger things. Remember: you can do "everything through Christ, who gives [you] strength" (Philippians 4:13).

Challenge: If you are dealing with depression or any other mental illness, please speak to someone immediately. If you know someone dealing with these issues, offer a hand and let him or her know you are there to listen and help.

Discussion Questions

1. When you hear *mental illness*, what comes into your mind?

2. Do you know someone struggling with mental illness? How do you know he or she is?

3. What kind of advice would you give someone struggling with mental illness?

4. Why do you think our community is reluctant to speak about mental illness?

5. If you were to go through depression or other forms of mental illness, what platforms are available to you to get help?

CHAPTER 9

Parents Are from Mars and Children Are from Venus

Are they always telling you to do things you don't want to do? No, I don't mean the voices in your head. I am talking about your parents. It's hard to believe you are even related to them. Don't you sometimes wish you could get one big trap to make them go away? (For your safety and everyone's around you, pls dnt.)

I've seen it over and over, and as I said, I've had to deal with this myself. No matter how rough it gets, the reality is this: They are your parents and you do have to live with them. More importantly, listening to and obeying our parents is a Christian obligation. I hope to shed some light on this subject to make your life (and the lives of your parents) a little easier.

This Journey Is Mine

As I was getting ready to battle one of the biggest spiritual wars of my life before heading to the monastery, a different type of battle was brewing between my dad and me. The moment I told him I was going to quit my job and pursue a different journey for my life, my dad and I could not get along. He thought my decision was irrational. Although he wanted me to serve God, he did not want me to do so like this. He thought it was extreme. At the same time I thought he was getting in the way of my relationship with God.

At this point in my life I didn't want anything to deter me from what I knew was a calling from God. My dad told me to stay in America, but in my heart I was already at the monastery. You see, my dad did not want me to be financially distressed (years later I learned that ignoring his concerns had been a huge mistake). We not only disagreed, but on the night right before I left, we had a heated discussion. I told him that he could not tell me what to do. I was an adult and he was treating me like a child! I had planned the trip down to the last detail in such a way that I was not going to be finically dependent on my parents. I was not asking them for money, and I was not asking for their help. Truthfully, I was not even asking for their blessing. In fact, my initial plan was to write a note that read something like this:

> Dear Mom & Dad:
>
> I love you and thank you for all you have done. Now I must answer the call of God. I am heading to a monastery.
>
> In Jesus's name,
>
> Dawit

But I did not write the note. I could only imagine the look on their faces if they had read a note like that! I regretted not writing it, but now I realize the argument was a bad one. I told my dad, "I don't need your money or approval! I am pursuing the will of God and I am not doing anything wrong." And so I went.

Rock Bottom: Coming Home

Without getting into the specifics, by the time I came back from the monastery, all the money I had saved was gone. I had a total of $0.00 in the bank account. All that boasting about how I had planned my life—and here I was. I had lost my car, house, money, everything! I hit rock bottom. I wondered how I would face my friends and family, but more importantly, how was I going to face my dad? I mean, I had told him I did not need him. What was he going to say to me?

Well, my dad did not say anything. Instead, the second day after I came back, he took me to a car dealership and bought me a new car! I learned a lot from this experience. I know you may not think so now, but your parents care about you more than anyone else in your life. The reason they yell and scream at times is because they do not want you to fall and hit "rock bottom." But if you do, they will always be there to lift you up.

Understanding Them: Mission Impossible

Parents speak a different language—and I don't mean Amharic. Our parents grew up in a time where things were vastly different. Accordingly, those experiences have shaped them to think a particular way.

Next time you get a chance, sit down with your parents and ask them about their childhood. Most people our age would simply tell you about their friends, school, and maybe other extracurricular activities they were involved in. But not our parents! They begin with the dramatic story of walking four miles to school each day, transition to how difficult life was at that time, and conclude with an emotional discourse about politics. But if you are able to really listen to their stories, you will see how they were able to endure many trials and overcome hardships. Despite all the trials, they prevailed. They worked hard and managed to have a successful life back in Ethiopia.

Here in America, however, the hard work and such would be considered the true "success story" or "American dream." Your parents may have achieved a certain level of comfort in Ethiopia, but because they love you, they gave all that up to come here and drive a taxi. Why? To give you better opportunities, of course! They didn't come to America for themselves. They came here so you would have access to education. They were hoping for you to be academically strong and have a great and healthy relationship with God.

School Days

As you know, your parents can get frustrated with you the moment you decide to stop studying. They did not have the luxury of having their own schoolbooks to take home. They had to wait in line for several hours at the library. Once they were able to get the textbook in their hands, they had a limited amount of time to study the chapters they needed for class. Now when you have an unlimited number of resources at your fingertips and you are not using them, your parents are left in dismay. They can't help but think how much they would have taken advantage of such an opportunity.

Our parents are also victims of the Red Terror era. For those of you who may not know, this was a period when thousands of Ethiopians were massacred during the Derg regime. During this time many of your parents' friends and family were either killed or arrested. Your parents themselves may have been arrested.

Think about the psychological effect this life-changing event can have on a person. If you ask your parents, you will learn that this was a very scary time for them. People would leave their houses not knowing if they were going to come back safely. It was a terrifying time for them. I am not a psychologist, but I believe this fear has caused the overly protective nature of our parents. A simple request to spend the night at a friend's house can result in unwarranted concerns and fears from your parents. For example, I recall my mama telling me that I couldn't order pizza because she thought the pizza delivery guy would kill me. I was sixteen at the time *smh*. I just couldn't believe it!

Here's the thing: Even though you don't agree with your parents, you must try to understand them. Their overly protective nature is a manifestation of their deep love for you. Ironically, we tend to get more annoyed by our parents' care the older we get. One would think the older we get the more understanding we would be about their good intentions, but that is not the case. I've noticed that a lot of young professionals tend to respond with a level of disrespect toward their parents' affection. Our parents' calling multiple times in a day to check up on us (or worrying about the vacation we plan to take in a remote part of the world) are all signs of how much they love us.

Don't shun them and get annoyed. Be thankful you have loving parents!

L.I.S.T.E.N. (How to Win an Argument with Your Parents)

Do you feel as if your voice is never heard? Do you feel you can never win an argument with your parents? Well, here is what you should do: L.I.S.T.E.N.! Trust me. By following the steps listed below, you are bound to have a better relationship with your parents. Good news is, these steps are not age restricted, so even if you are grown but still find yourself in a pickle with your parents, you can apply the L.I.S.T.E.N. acronym to your life. It looks like this:

L.I.S.T.E.N.

Look at the time

Improve your grades

Sit them down

Take control

Escape

"No" means "no"

L: Look at the Time. The biggest mistake you can make when arguing with your parents is not getting the timing correct. Remember: there is always a time and a place for things. The first way you can win with your parents is to predict when they will most likely be in a good mood. If you want to ask them if you may spend the night at a friend's house during the weekend, the best time to do it is not when they first come home after a long day at work (or the first thing in the morning for that matter). I remember my dad used to tell me never to ask for anything until he finished eating dinner. If you've ever had a job—especially if you're a little older—you should be able to understand this point. How do you feel after getting off work? Chances are that your parents are not in a good mood when they first get home from work; thus, they will not give you the type of answer you are looking for. Remember, friends—everyone needs some time to decompress. The last thing you want to do is get in a shouting match with your parents right after they've put in a long, stressful day.

Another timing issue is to avoid bringing up a controversial subject in a middle of an argument. This is perhaps the biggest mistake young adults make when communicating with their parents. If you don't know what I am talking about, consider the following example. Meet Shate'quiena.

Shate'quiena is seventeen years old and is planning to meet up with her friends after school. There will not be alcohol or drugs where she is planning to go, so in her mind she does not see a problem with going. On her way out, however, her dad tells her she can't leave the house because it is already too late.

Most girls (and boys) in this situation would get into a shouting match with their parents. But this is the wrong way to handle it. I guarantee that if you start shouting, you will not win the argument! So what do you do? It is simple: Let it go.

I will repeat it again in case you missed it: *Let it go!* For dramatic purposes, just one more time: **Let it go!** Once your parents have decided, you should know that this will be their final answer. There is no reason for you to throw a tantrum and argue with them because arguing and throwing tantrums will not solve the issue. There will be other times your friends will get together and other opportunities for you to go out with them, so be smart and sit this one out. No serious conversations can ever take place while emotions are high. With your mind on going out that night, you are likely not going to be able to articulate your points in a meaningful manner. Accept the reality, as bitter as it may be, and stay home. Listening to your parents in a time like that will actual prove to them that you are more mature than they think. The next time this kind of thing happens, you will be more likely to get your way. Finally, once the emotions are gone, you can calmly talk to them about being able to see your friends (see the "Sit Them Down" step for details).

I: Improve Your Grades. Most of the time your parents restrict you from doing anything because your grades are not where they need to be. The better you do at school, the less likely your parents are going to give you a hard time at home. Parents believe meeting up with friends, watching TV, and playing video games—anything you may consider "fun"—are distractions from school. Thus, if you continue to improve in your schoolwork, they will have little reason to say no to you since there is no evidence you are being distracted from improving and learning.

If your grades are already where they need to be, there is probably some other way your parents want you to improve.

For example, the older you get the more your parents are going to want to spend time with you. This is especially true if you are currently in college. During the school year they never see you because you consistently have to study. For this reason they look forward to the winter and summer breaks to spend time with you. However, if you spend each weekend away at a friend's house, your parents will begin to complain. Learn to say no to your friends from time to time and spend more time with your parents. Do so voluntarily. This will go a long way! I promise—the world will not stop if you spend one Friday night with your parents. Take them out. Show them a good time. I know that sounds a little funny, but now that you are grown, your parents should be more of a friend than just an authority figure. Plus, the more time you spend with them, the less stressful your life will be.

Finally, taking the initiative to be with them—as well as doing things for them like cleaning when you're at home—will prove to them you're growing up and maturing. The more you can show them you are responsible and mature, the more freedom they will give you.

S: Sit Them Down. As we already discussed, choosing the right time to talk to your parents is critical in winning an argument. This does not mean avoiding important conversations altogether, but it does mean avoiding important conversations at certain times of the day. Thus, part of having a successful argument with your parents is setting the mood. For example, every young girl dreams of the day her Prince Charming bends the knee and asks her hand in marriage. What makes this event so desirable is not just the question but also all the events tied up with the big question.

Think about it this way. If a young man texts his girlfriend and asks, "Wanna get married?" what is the likelihood the girl will say yes? On the other hand, if the same young man buys flowers, takes her to the place they first met, waits until the stars are shining, and gets on his knee to ask her, "Will you marry me?" how will she respond? Clearly he has a better chance with the latter approach.

The same thing is true with your parents. Set the mood properly. "Romance" them a little! Do something generous around the house: clean, cook, be nice, volunteer to do something extra. Not just for one night, but really try to get this going for a while. Show a pattern so they don't think you're up to something. Then let them know you want to have a serious conversation with them and schedule a time in advance. This is key, people! You need to schedule important, especially controversial, conversations in advance so both parties can mentally prepare.

Ideally, you should be scheduling time with your parents at least once a week. If you set aside some time proactively, then you'll discover that all the things causing you guys to fight and argue about disappear. Hence, you can enjoy the rest of the time you have with your parents without having to argue or fight about anything. Whenever an issue arises, you will both know there is a dedicated time to talk about those things so you can avoid arguing every chance you get.

T: Take Control. Be honest. Does your voice enter a high-register pitch and sound like an old cat being choked every time you begin to argue? Are you one of those people who gets overly emotional when talking about the most trivial matter? If so, you need to learn how to control your emotions.

My parents told me recently that when I was growing up there were many occasions when they wanted to say yes to something I asked for but ended up saying no just because of the way I was acting. Think about it. If you were a parent, would you allow your teenage kid to get behind the wheel of a car after throwing a tantrum around the house? If people are not able to control their emotions, how in the world are they going to control a car?

Controlling your emotions is important not only when dealing with your parents—it is a good practice for all parts of your life. You must learn how to engage in a conversation that makes you feel uncomfortable without screaming and yelling. The first thing you need to do is to take control of your voice. Don't allow it to reach that high pitch. You know what I'm talking about. If you hear your voice going up like that, this is the sign that you're getting upset, so monitor your feelings. If you notice your emotions getting the best of you, simply ask your parents if you may be excused. Take a few minutes to compose yourself and cool down. Once you are able to calm yourself, go back and finish the conversation.

Story time: A few years ago I was having an intense meeting with my boss. He was accusing me of "bamboozling" (his words) him to avoid doing work. That could not have been farther from the truth. I had sent him multiple emails letting him know the project assigned to me needed further explanation, and I could not work on it until he provided me with the needed information. Midway into the meeting my boss became extremely disrespectful. I was trying to explain my position the best way I knew how, but he became more and more erratic. At that point I felt disrespected and angry. I could feel my blood pressure rising by the minute. Since

I knew responding in anger would not resolve anything, I calmly asked him if we could both take a few minutes to cool down and then reconvene. He agreed, and we halted the meeting. When we came back for the meeting he was completely different. Not only did he apologize numerous times but he also ended up doing most of the work on the project and gave me credit for it. ☺Now, that is what I call taking control!

E: Escape. As reminded by the great Aretha Franklin, all people are asking for is a little respect.[20] It is true. We all want to be respected by everyone, but even more so by our parents. Even if you keep getting into trouble and into arguments with your parents, you can get away with a lot of it as long you are able to show them respect.

Let's flip the script. Imagine one fine morning you find yourself being the sole caregiver of someone close to you. You are given the task of bathing, feeding, clothing, and taking him or her out for a walk. This person you care for has mood swings, so the job description requires you to cradle the person when he or she cries and continuously try to make the person laugh by playing with him or her. But the worst thing of all, you even have to wipe the person's poop! How long do you think you can do this? Two days? Maybe a week or so? Let's say you have extreme self-control and hold out for three years. Suddenly the person you've been caring for is better, actually cured. But now that the person is better, if he or she starts to randomly scream, curse, and disrespect you, what would you think? You would probably call him or her an ungrateful brat!

Well, this is similar to the feeling your parents have whenever

---

[20] See Otis Redding, "Respect" (Steve Cropper, 1965).

you talk back to them. If anything, your parents have been putting up with your nonsense—your disrespect—for your *whole life*, so they have the right to be frustrated. If you don't know what qualifies as being disrespectful, here are just a few examples:

- Rolling your eyes
- Yelling back at them
- Looking at your phone while they are talking
- Having earphones in your ears when they talk
- Slamming your door after a conversation
- Storming out of the house while they are talking
- Not responding to them when they talk to you
- Throwing a tantrum (stomping your feet, waving your hands around, gesticulating)
- Comparing yourself with your parents ("Why can't I do it if you did it?")

This is not an exhaustive list, but it's a good start. If I had to name the big one, in my opinion being on your phone with your earphones in your ears when they talk to you is a huge sign of disrespect. That is equivalent to telling your parents what they have to say is not as important as whatever it is you are doing on your phone. You can do better, dude! Imagine if someone did that to you when you were trying to discuss something important. You wouldn't like that to happen to you, so don't do it to others. The Golden Rule, baby.

FYI . . . honoring our parents is a Christian obligation. It is not just a mere "good" thing to do, but God expects this from us. As you know, we must respect God at all times:

> "Therefore, the Lord, the God of Israel, says: I promised that your branch of the tribe of Levi would always be my priests. But I will honor those who honor me, and I will despise those who think lightly of me." (1 Samuel 2:30)

We honor God by fulfilling our obligations to Him and respecting the things He respects. Make sense? Good! Now consider the fifth commandment: "Honor your father and mother. Then you will live a long, full life in the land the Lord your God is giving you" (Exodus 20:12). Notice that this is a commandment, not a suggestion. And there is no age restriction on this. Even if you are grown with kids of your own, you still have to respect to your parents—regardless of how "annoying" you think they are!

Let me mention this: the more you grow up, the more you will find yourself disagreeing with your parents on a variety of issues. That is part of life! You have to learn how to communicate effectively with them. Remember: this does not give you the right to treat them badly.

N: "No" Means "No." The last thing you should remember is that your parents are still your parents. Don't try to compete with them when they tell you what to do. To put it another way, you have to know your place, boo boo. You have the right to ask them why they told you to do something. You can even disagree with their decisions, but you must respect and honor what they tell you.

Understand: your parents are not your friends. They are your parents. Part of that relationship is being able to understand that they make decisions on your behalf. You may not like it, but that is the reality.

Once you grow up you will find yourself in a similar situation with your boss. You can go to work and request certain things to take place, but at the end of the day your boss has the final say. That's just the reality of life. The sooner you accept your reality, the easier your life will get and the less you will have to fight with your parents.

Your parents are your biggest supporters. No one in this world will ever care for you as much as they do. They are on your team. Don't spend all your energy fighting with someone on your team! If you find yourself constantly arguing with your parents, you are doing something wrong. Especially if you are still living at home, figure out a better way to communicate with them. The constant arguing is impacting you in more ways than you think.

I will leave you with this final thought: If you haven't caught up yet, the step to winning an argument is to L.I.S.T.E.N. to your parents. Be calm. Be cool. Use your ears: if you are sitting down with you parents expecting them to understand your point of view, you have to be ready to listen to what they are saying too. Don't be too stubborn. Learn how to compromise. Even if you don't get everything you want, if your parents are trying to work with you to fix a problem, give in a little and compromise. The more you L.I.S.T.E.N. the more you will resolve your issues.

Challenge: Write a letter to your parents letting them know how much you love them. The letter should include all the great things they have done for you over the years and should *not* include any issues or problems you guys have. Keep it uplifting.

Discussion Questions

1. Describe your relationship with your parents.

2. Describe an incident with your parents when you did (or said) something wrong to them. How did you react? Did you apologize?

3. What aspect of this relationship do you wish could be improved/changed?

4. What element(s) of L.I.S.T.E.N. do you already practice at home?

5. What element(s) of L.I.S.T.E.N. do you think will be hard to implement? Why?

CHAPTER 10

I Wanna Be a Deacon... I Think

So you think you may want to be a deacon. But why? Have you ever asked yourself why you want to be a deacon? What would the benefits be? Before you continue reading, please take about ten minutes to really think about this and write down your answer.

The Reasoning

Well, what is your reasoning? If you said to better serve God, I have some good news for you—you don't have to be a deacon to do that! We are all called to serve God with the special talents He has given us, but not everyone is cut out to be a deacon. Let's look into this.

The mind-set of being a deacon should be that of a person seeking to be a slave. As crazy as it may seem, that is what deaconhood is all about. The word *deacon* is a Greek-based word that closely translates to being a servant—as in a slave of God. Therefore, if you are in the process of getting ordained, I urge you to take time to really consider if this is something you want to pursue. Then after you've prayed and gone through a process of discernment, if you still have a strong desire to become a deacon, my advice is to extend your day of ordination by one year. I know this may seem excessive, but this is the best way to test if your yearning is being generated from your emotions or if it is a fire burning inside you.

Making Sense of the Emotions

A few years ago I had a strong burning desire to become a slave to God. However, I could not discern if the feeling inside me was just another emotion making me feel this way or if it was the Holy Spirit urging me to follow Him. Since I knew this was a lifetime commitment, I decided to wait two years before deciding. In those two years the feeling intensified. There was nothing on my mind except this strong urge pulling me toward service. Eventually I surrendered to the Holy Spirit and started my journey to Ethiopia, where I was ordained.

In my case there was not one day when I said the words "I want to be a deacon." In fact, there were many opportunities presented to me wherein I could have easily been ordained. However, my agreement with God was to prepare myself for whatever service He wished me to pursue. Getting ordained was His plan—not mine or my parents'.

The truth is, there is no shortage of deacons within the Church. Over the last few years we have seen a surge in the number of deacons. I would say instead that we have a shortage of Christians. That's right! Our Church needs more Christians who actually live by the Word of God. We need more people who are honest and righteous, always striving to bring honor to God's name. Anyone can stand and repeat a chant he has studied, but it is extremely difficult to live our lives according to the will of God. If you really want to serve the Church, start with striving to be a good Christian. This is what the Church needs today.

External Pressure

Sometimes parents are the driving force behind their children getting ordained. Is that your case? Do you feel your parents are forcing you to become a deacon? If not your parents, is it a clergy member from the church? If that is the case, speak up now. Deaconhood is a lifetime commitment, and you should not allow yourself to make this great commitment without being sure of your desire. If your parents or others do not listen to you the first time around, keep telling them over and over again.

How Do I Know If I'm Ready?

When addressing Saint Timothy, Saint Paul outlined some key characteristics a deacon must possess. If you are considering becoming a deacon, ask yourself if you fulfill the requirements:

> Also, people outside the church must speak well of him so that he will not be disgraced and fall into the devil's trap. In the same way, deacons must be well respected and have integrity. They must not be heavy drinkers or dishonest with money. (1 Timothy 3:7–8)

Notice how Saint Paul phrased this statement. Ask yourself—are your actions worthy of respect or are they worthy of condemnation? Each action you take will naturally cause others to react to it. The issue for deacons is that once they are ordained as deacons, their actions are a reflection of the Church.

A Real, True-Life Example

Consider the following example: When I say, "Catholic priest," what is the first thing that pops into your head? Be honest. You think about the scandals revolving pedophilia. Can you provide three Catholic priests' names who have been convicted of this crime? Chances are that you will not be able to, but you associate the entire priesthood with something so awful because of the actions of a few. The truth is that hundreds—if not thousands—of Catholic priests live a righteous and moral life and have no connection with such heinous behavior. Unfortunately, that is not how the rest of the world feels about it. Regardless of how much the Catholic Church tries to change its image, the actions of those few will forever remain a shadow casting doubts in the hearts of many followers.

The same thing is true with deacons. Once you begin to do something bad, especially in the public domain, no one will remember who you are. However, everyone will remember that "some deacon" behaved in a manner not worthy of respect. The more that deacons behave in a negative way, the more that deaconship will be linked with bad behavior. Therefore, because of the acts of a few the entire church will get a bad name.

The Deacon with Two Faces

Our Church is not immune from generalizations. Like Catholic priests, in some ways our Church might be facing a similar type of issue. With the recent surge of deacons in America, we are also seeing the formation of a new culture: deacons (often in their mid-teens) showing two different faces.

They wear the first face when they come into the church. They act and say all the things that would make them appear "righteous" in front of the congregation. They learn how to speak the Christian language ("Amen," "Thank you," God bless you," and so on). They quickly gain the trust of the Church priests and leaders.

The second face comes out the moment they leave the church. Suddenly all that holiness and righteousness leaves their soul faster than Usain Bolt sprinting during a race. The Christian language is then replaced with #$@&%*! this and #$@&%*! that. Instead of following the Holy Spirit, they become too busy following girls. The worst part of it all is that they post all this nonsense on social media for the world to see.

Many people are beginning to leave the Orthodox Church because they think clergy are hypocrites. To put it another way, after seeing the actions of the two-faced deacons, people have left the house of God. This isn't to say that there are not many honorable deacons who are living a righteous life. But once again, the action of a few is causing many to have a negative view of young deacons. This is a serious problem that needs immediate attention, and there are some things you can do to help.

If you are a deacon (or not), the very least you can do to help change this negative image is to clean up your social media. What do you gain by showing the world all the sins you commit? Do you really want to honor your church? Or your deaconship for that matter? Then delete anything online that is not appropriate. If you are not sure what is appropriate, ask your mama. She'll tell you.

We All Change, Friend

It's not only about social media, however. You yourself must change. After all, this is the criteria for becoming a deacon. You have to respect the office of deaconship before you can expect others to respect it. Once you become a deacon, you are held to a higher standard. If you have not already, read the life of Saint Stephen; imitate his life and you'll be golden.

If you didn't get it before, I will say it again. Once you choose to be a deacon, you give up your right to a private life. You don't have the luxury of being like everybody else, enjoying your life any way you want. You must remember that you will always—no matter what you're up to—be a deacon. For example, you should not only avoid "much wine" but also avoid places where "much wine" is served (no wild parties and bars).

Let go of that life, my brother. Let it go! It is not worth it. Deaconhood is eternal, and your partying days are limited to just a few years here on earth. Do you really want to bring dishonor to your eternal office of clergy just to have "fun" with people you most likely will never see again? If you're not sure that the places you're going to are appropriate, take your mamma with you. She'll be able to tell you. Remember—if you don't feel comfortable taking your mother with you, why would you feel comfortable taking the two protecting angels constantly by your side into a place like that?

While we're on it, to the deacons who smoke weed . . . stop it! What a shame we even have to talk about this! So again I ask, how much do you want your deaconhood? Handling a deaconship is like handling an egg—you have to tender it with care. The slightest mishap can cause it to crack. After all, a cracked egg will never be the same. Don't be a fool. Repent of your sins. Why are you waiting? Do it now! Don't let the sun set before you complete this task.

So What Do I Get?

The primary gain you should be pursuing as a deacon is the one received from Christ. Each Sunday you wake up early and go to church there is a heavenly reward waiting for you. This should be the driving force and motivation behind your services.

There are also earthly gains that might come as a result of your services. As you might have already noticed, some clergy are compensated for their services. There is nothing wrong with getting paid; actually there is biblical precedent for that.

> For Scripture says, "Do not muzzle an ox while it is treading out the grain," and "The worker deserves his wages." (1 Timothy 5:18 NIV)

There is nothing wrong with being paid for the service. The problem arises when the motivation to serve becomes attached to financial gains—or being "dishonest with money" (1 Timothy 3:8). You must be committed to avoid the error of "pursuing dishonest gain" (NIV). The dishonesty occurs when your love of money overshadows your love of serving God. This is dishonest since you are no longer serving with a yearning to receive the eternal glory that awaits you. Instead, you are seeking temporal, earthly benefits. It is dishonest because you have bamboozled the congregation to believe that you are there to serve God when really you are there to serve yourself. Take heed, brother! Money is more addictive than wine. If you allow it to consume your mind, you will be drunk with greed.

The Root of All Evil?

Money is not the only dishonest gain, however. Vainglory (ውዳሴ ከንቱ) is perhaps as destructive, if not more destructive, than the love of money. Vainglory is the result of someone being over-glorified to the point where the person thinks he or she is better than everyone else. One time I heard a sermon stating that when the devil cannot get you to do bad things, he gets you to do good. Why? Because once you begin to do good works, people will come and glorify you instead of glorifying our deserving God. This inevitably leads you to be overly prideful. Thus, the fall behind vainglory is much more damaging than falling in wicked actions.

When it comes to wicked actions, at least you are cognizant of the fact that your actions are deplorable in the eyes of God. This realization hopefully will drive you to a repentant heart. Under the cloud of vainglory, however, you are not able to see your wrong doings. For example, when I first started giving sermons, I fell into this trap. When people told me I gave "good sermons," I started thinking that I was good. The reality is this: all the gifts I have come from God.

The minute I forget this reality is the minute God's grace will leave me.

You can easily tell if you are guilty of this weakness by assessing your first thoughts after service. What is the first thing you usually do after preaching a sermon or doing Kidase? Do you thank God for allowing you to serve in His name? Or do you try to find out what people thought about it? A person who suffers from this temptation will first walk around the church eavesdropping on conversations to see if anyone is commenting on his service. If he can't find anyone to speak or compliment his style of service, he will then approach someone and ask what his or her favorite part of the service was. He hopes the person will respond by saying, "*Your* service!" If he doesn't get the response he seeks, he will ask openly, "How was my . . . [sermon, Kidase, *kebero,* and so on]?" At this moment the devil declares his victory.

Having a Clear Conscience

I bring this up to warn you of the temptations that await you as you begin to serve the Church. The younger you are the more accolades you are likely to receive from your congregation. Seriously, try not to pay attention to those. Focusing on this praise will cause you to eventually fall and forget about God—the one who enabled you to be in this position. Remember—we must "keep hold of the deep truths of the faith with a clear conscience" (1 Timothy 3:9 NIV). Being a deacon means so much more than being able to do Kidase on Sundays. You have to also know and "hold . . . truths of the faith." As a deacon you are the face of the Orthodox Church. Furthermore, if someone were to ask you to explain your faith, you must be able to do so. How much time have you spent learning about the deep, beautiful, mysterious teachings of the Church?

As they say (don't ask me who), the teachings of the Church are vast and can never be completed. Nonetheless, you can continue to gain understanding and knowledge of the Church. The more you learn about the Church the more you will fall in love with it. For example, think about a husband and a wife. When they were dating they declared their love for each other after they had a chance to get to know each other. After marriage, the more they learn about each other the more they fall in love. In the same way, you cannot fully love your church until you take time to learn about it. And what does a person do when he or she falls in love?—declare it to the world! The person posts it on social media and tells his or her friends and family. The same thing is true with the Church. Only when you truly fall in love can you become an ambassador of the Church and teach others about it. Set time aside for yourself to learn more about your church.

At the risk of getting hit by a *mekwamia* (መቋሚያ) by the old-timers, let me just say learning about the Church does *not* mean memorizing a bunch of prayers in *Ge'ez*. Memorizing prayers like *Wedase Mariam* (a prayer book used within the Church) is extremely useful for service and is expected of a deacon. However, that memorization does not substitute for learning about the Church. Learning about your faith means being able to understand the complex teachings of the Triune God, the hypostatic union, the formula of miaphysitism, the transubstantiation of the Eucharist, and the hope found in the studies of eschatology. Without understanding these principles, one cannot claim to know the Church.

Ugh! Too Much Pressure! I Can't Do This Anymore!

Are you beginning to feel frustrated with church service? Are you feeling overwhelmed? Do you feel as if many people are expecting too much from you? You want me to hold your arm and sing *"eshi ru-ru"* as your mommy did? Should I get you a milk bottle while we are at it?

Come on, man! You are a soldier of Christ! Soldiers do not have time to warm up their milk bottles in a battle. Yes, things can get difficult, but you must keep going. How do you think a real soldier is able to get up and keep fighting when his life is at risk? You know what is at stake here. Therefore, like any good soldier, it is better to die fighting than not to fight at all. Remember that you are a member of the heavenly army of soldiers fighting for the cause of Christ. You can endure any trials that come along your way. There is a reward waiting for you. God sees every attempt you make throughout your service. From the small trials to the big ones, God sees you. Keep moving forward and keep "fighting the good fight" (1 Timothy 6:12 NIV).

Behind the "Curtain"

So now that you're still considering becoming a deacon, I thought I would provide you with some of the most common issues many deacons face today. These are in no particular order of priority, but each must be considered.

TeNsi- tenSI-Tensi-TENSsssIUu leselot! Do you remember doing *Kidase* for the first time? Each time your part came, you couldn't start on the right note and had to keep on starting over until you got it right. Maybe you are still on this part of your service. Isn't it embarrassing—messing up in front of the congregation? When you look to the side, you may even see a few people laughing at you. Your heart begins to beat fast, your hands start to shake, and your voice just can't hit the right notes. Or even worse, you forget the words in mid-Kidase! Have you been left on stage feeling ridiculed? If you have experienced such things, you are probably the only one who cares. The congregation pays little attention to such mishaps. Yes, they may notice or even make a few comments here and there, but that's about it.

The truth is that you're not as important as you think you are! A few mistakes here and there are not the end of the world. Even the best priests make mistakes. It's part of life. As the saying goes, "Practice makes perfect." Don't let the negative comments deter you from serving God. The good news is that God does not look for a perfect voice; he looks for a perfect heart. You should be seeking God's approval, not man's. If you approach service with a pure heart, who cares what people say? All you need to know is that your service is being accepted by God. And as I already said, nobody is paying close attention to you anyhow. It's all in your head. Clear your mind and continue to serve God. Don't let these small things get in the way of your service.

"Is This What You've Been Learning at Church?" Have your parents ever said this to you after you've done something bad? So annoying! Sometimes it can get so frustrating that you may want to quit being a deacon, but don't! As frustrating as it is, deep down inside you know they are right. Yes, you are still young and desire to do the same things as your friends, but you have a bigger responsibility. Perhaps your parents are urging you more and more to study Kidase or to read your Bible, but this should not frustrate you. After all, they are doing this for your benefit.

If you feel your parents' expectations are a bit high, simply have a conversation with them. A conversation means a conversation—not a shouting match! Show them that you are mature and can have an adult conversation. Put away the games, turn off the TV, sit them down, and calmly (stress on *calmly*) explain why you think their expectations are a bit too high. Your parents are a lot more reasonable than you think (see the chapter 9 section on "L.I.S.T.E.N.").

If you are feeling overwhelmed by the responsibilities of the Church, take a step back and evaluate your life. Are you really overwhelmed or is that an excuse? Do you really have no time for yourself or do you just want to spend more time with your friends? These are questions only you can answer, but a wise priest once told me, "ቤተክርስቲያን ሰው የላትም," which roughly translates into "The Church does not have people." At the time I didn't understand what he meant. After all, there were hundreds, if not thousands, of people going to church every Sunday. Over the years I started to see what he meant. Especially for this new English-speaking generation, no one is willing to dedicate his or her time and energy to them. There is so much work to be done but no one to do it. Therefore, I urge you to dedicate yourself, especially if you are in a position to make a change at your local church. Do it! Yes, it requires dedication and sacrifice, but that's what being a deacon is all about. You will see how satisfying it is when God rewards you. Lord knows, I wanted to walk away from this service many times. But through the grace of God and many, many, many words of advice from the amazing mentors around me, I stuck it out. Now when I see my students grown up and serving in the church, I take great pride in that. Now I know that each moment I sacrificed was worth it.

Oh, No—He Didn't! When you first started serving the Church, you probably thought everyone around you was holy and incapable of making mistakes. I remember a young man once asked me, "Do priests sin?" This question represents the mind-set many deacons have when they enter the Church. You soon discover this is an erroneous way of thinking and that priests, like any other person, are also prone to making mistakes. Since you may look at the priest as your role model, the first time you see him doing something inappropriate you may be devastated. Plus, when you are exposed to people you respect and look up to doing shady things, many times you will lose hope in your church. I have personally talked to many deacons who have decided to stop serving the Church because of the actions of a few priests. But remember—leaving the Church does not solve anything!

If you find yourself in a middle of such a scenario, you must understand that there is a right way and a wrong way to handle it. The *wrong* thing to do is leave the Church. If anything, there won't be anyone else there to correct the issue, and the problems you witnessed will only continue to worsen.

Another wrong way to handle this is by being disrespectful to the priest or authority you have an issue with. Someone doing something improper does not give you a free ticket to say and do whatever you wish—especially if you are a deacon in your late teens to early twenties. Yes, I am talking to you! Your age category is known as the "fire" age. It causes you to act on emotions rather than reason. You must learn how to control your emotions. I cannot emphasize this enough—everything you do must be out of love and respect. Respecting our elders is a not conditional advice but rather a commandment that remains true under all circumstances.

Finally, the worst way to handle witnessing inappropriate behavior is attempting to "expose" the wrong doings of the priest. Under no circumstances should you do this. This was Ham's mistake after seeing his father, Noah, drunk on the vineyard (see Genesis 8:20–24). Do you not know that the priest is still your father, even if he makes a mistake? What benefit is there in shaming your father? I guarantee you, doing that will only cause more division and altercations in your church. You will lose credibility and will not have a platform where you can spread your message. Don't waste your energy trying to do tasks that are useless and bring no success.

Dude, That Wasn't Cool; So What Should I Do? The right way to deal with trials is first to pray. Prayer gives the Holy Spirit an opportunity to get involved. You are more likely to overcome these trials you are facing by trusting the Holy Spirit by your side than by trying to do it alone.

Second, stay in your lane! Remember the passage from the Luke that reads, "If you are faithful in little things, you will be faithful in large ones. But if you are dishonest in little things, you won't be honest with greater responsibilities" (16:10). Right now you are entrusted with the little things— the small matters. Show yourself to be worthy of the matters delegated to you. Before you wave your finger around at others and accuse them of doing their job incorrectly, ask yourself if you have been faithful in the responsibilities you have been given. I know this seems harsh, but that is what we are asked to do.

Now I must also point this out to you: If someone is getting in the way of your service and asking you to do something improper, speak up! Speak firmly but speak with love! You do not have to get involved in something you feel is dishonest or immoral. You can speak boldly as Saint Stephen did when he stood before his trial (see Acts 6–7), but this should be your last resort. Before then you can ask to speak with those in authority and explain to them why you feel these actions are against your values. Is there a chance you misunderstood their motives? Can it be that you are being too emotional? Take time to evaluate the situation before you do anything.

Storytime

Once upon a time there was a bishop praying his daily prayer outside a church. Out of nowhere a young boy came running to the priest, crying and complaining that the other deacons were fighting inside the sanctuary. The bishop looked at him and said, "Why don't you go inside and fix it?" Through this statement the bishop was relaying two points. The first one was much more immediate to the boy's request. He was simply urging the boy to go back inside and tell the deacons to stop fighting. This is a task the boy could have accomplished. There was no need to go to the bishop. From this we learn that there are tasks in the church we shouldn't wait for others to complete. We can simply go in and "fix" them ourselves.

The second meaning requires much more patience and time. When he said, "Go in," he meant it in a symbolic sense of getting closer into the services of the church. In a sense he was telling him to become a deacon (thereby coming closer to service) and through his actions show other deacons how to behave in a sanctuary. This way he would be able to fix the behavior of the deacons in a more systematic and long-lasting way.

Furthermore, the bishop's word meant for the boy to grow in service to the point of priesthood. At this level he could make a greater impact by teaching deacons and having better control over their behavior in the sanctuary.

Last, his words urged the young boy to surrender his life to the services of the Church by becoming a bishop. Through this office he could have full authority and power to make the positive changes he wished to make.

I will leave you with this: Even if you may not seek to be a bishop, or even a priest for that matter, seek to grow in your services. If you truly want to make changes and impact the lives of many people in a way that matters, get into the Church and fix it, brothers! This is the only way!

Challenge: Write a one-page paper on the teachings of the Ethiopian Orthodox Church and post it on social media. If you do not have social media, share it with family and friends. Be sure to let a clergy member review your paper before posting it.

Discussion Questions

1. Why do/did you want to become a deacon?

2. What are the biggest challenges deacons face?

3. How do deacons deal with temptations?

4. How often do deacons meet with their Confession Father?

5. Do you have social media? If so, have you ever posted something on it you should have not posted?

CHAPTER 11

What's Next?

Y ou've nearly reached the end of this book. Since you've come this far, I'm guessing you're ready to be a full-blown, dedicated Orthodox junky! Well, maybe not a junky, but did you at least learn something? We have covered many topics, and I pray you've been able to see just how intricate and mysterious the Ethiopian Orthodox Church is. Believe it or not, we barely scratched the surface! At any rate, I hope some of your questions about our Church were answered. More importantly, I hope you are beginning to see why your parents may seem critical about your not going to church every Sunday. I also hope you see the beautiful, majestic things the Church has to offer you. The Church is your mother, after all. Thus, I would like to leave you with some thoughts to consider.

Keep Learning

If we look at the Old Testament, we find a young man named Samuel. Samuel was sound asleep when God called him in the middle of the night. We read in the story that Samuel got up and walked over to a man named Eli, thinking it was his voice he had heard instead of God's. Eli told him he hadn't called the young man. Samuel returned to bed, and *again* God called him. And *again* Samuel got up, thinking it was Eli.[21]

Think about this for a moment. First of all, Habesha kids should be able to relate with this. Parents have this predisposition of randomly calling their kid's name for no apparent reason. Once the child comes asking what the parents want, the parent asks the child to fetch for them the TV remote control—which is always within hand's reach, *smh*. Maybe it's just me, but I digress . . .

The most fascinating thing about the story of Samuel is where it says "again." Samuel kept going back and forth between his bed and talking to Eli three times. It was on the fourth try that he was able to hear the voice of God. Case in point? You may have to keep going back and forth to church before discerning the voice of God from other voices in your head.[22]

---

21 1 Samuel 3:1–8
22 If you actually hear voices in your head, please put the book down and seek help immediately. Just saying.

Keep Coming Back

One trip to church is not going to change your life. Reading one book is not going to bring any substantial change to your spiritual life. You may have to go to church consistently several times to see the result. I'm a very logical person. If I had to reduce everything down to a formula it would be the following:

Hard Work + Consistency = Success

Most of the time we are willing to do one but not the other. For example, Steve Jobs worked hard. No doubt about that. His hard work enabled him to cofound Apple, Inc. He was also fired from Apple in 1985. This didn't stop him. In short, he worked harder and harder until (I guess you could say) he got his job back.[23] Can you imagine if he had given up? Today most people associate the name "Steve Jobs" with success, but to get to where he was, he had to work hard and be consistent. Similarly, Martin Luther King Jr., who is known for being one of the most influential speakers of all time, received a "C" in his . . . wait for it . . . public speaking class![24] Look at the best basketball player of all time. Michael Jordan didn't make the varsity team when he first tried out![25] The list continues. But can you imagine what this world would have looked like if these people had given up?

---

23 Walter Isaacson, *Steve Jobs* (Simon & Schuster, 2011).
24 Alyssa Shea, "Martin Luther King Jr. Barely Passed Public Speaking." November 4, 2018. *FAILURE: The Secret to Success*: https://www.failurethebook.com/2013/11/04/martin-luther-king-jr-barely-passed-public-speaking/.
25 "Michael Jordan Didn't Make Varsity—At First." *Newsweek Special Edition*, October 17, 2015. *Newsweek:* https://www.newsweek.com/missing-cut-382954.

I NEED ANSWERS

This formula also works in the spiritual realm. Take for example the inspiring story of Saint Yared. Growing up, he was not good at school. Many had given up on him, but he kept pushing forward. One day when he was frustrated about school, he saw a small insect attempting to climb a tree. The insect fell but got back up and started climbing the tree again. The insect repeated this process seven times before successfully climbing all the way to the top. Seeing this, young Yared was inspired. He thought, *If this insect can keep pushing forward and not be discouraged by its failure, I can also keep pushing forward. And if I fall . . . I can always just get back up.* It was this attitude that led him to be the pioneer of the Ethiopian Orthodox Tewahedo Church's chants (*zema*) and teachings. Finally he went on to be a scholar and set the foundation for the form of worship we use in our Church to this day.[26]

Hard work means you have to be willing to learn more about the Church to see a change in your spiritual life. Thus, if you are committed and ready to put in the work, I have included a resource section in the back of this book. Here you will find ideas for what to do next. By the way, I urge you to reread this book again and again to give yourself a chance to understand the many topics covered. Meditate on the chapters. Do the challenges at the end of the chapters repeatedly. See if your answers change to monitor how you've grown.

Remember—hard work must be coupled with consistency. Christianity is a way of life—not just a one-time action. You must be willing to change the way you live your life. This means that even the way you think must be transformed. This change can come only when you are willing to fully

---

26 *Hagiography of St. Yared* (Ethiopian Orthodix Tewahedo Church).

surrender your life to our Lord and Savior, Jesus Christ. Pray, learn, and grow!

Change Your Mind

One time at my college I was giving a sermon in Bible study about discovering God. The town was a college town, so we rarely came across anyone over the age of forty—and certainly not Ethiopians. Hence, you could imagine my dismay when two elderly Ethiopian women in their late sixties or early seventies suddenly popped into the Bible study. I couldn't believe what I was seeing! I kept on going with the sermon but all I could think about was how these two older women had just popped up out of nowhere! This went on for another minute or two, and then I heard myself say it: "Discover God before you are too old!" Everyone in the room was shocked by what I said, and so was I! The timing was uncanny and seemed extremely insensitive to the two women who had just walked in. But my words (action) resulted from my thought process. All I could think about was how old they were, so my thoughts ended up manifesting through my actions.

All this is to say—before looking to change your actions, change your mind. Decide today to live a better life with Christ. Also, remember what Saint Paul said when the church of Corinth was going through difficult times. He reminded the folks of Corinth to "be mature in understanding matters" (1 Corinthians 14:20). He didn't tell them just to be mature, but he told them to be mature in their thinking. If they were able to think in a mature fashion, then they would be able to act maturely as well. Don't worry about what actions you are going to change at this point in your life. God simply wants you to open up your heart for Him. Once you do that, the Holy Spirit will come in and transform your life.

Change Your Environment

Have you ever heard, "You are what you eat"? The same thing is true for your spiritual life. Just as your physical body needs physical food, your spiritual body needs spiritual food. If you surround yourself with negativity, you will not see your spiritual life growing. God by nature is holy; thus, He cannot be around sin. Conversely, the closer you are going toward sin and surrounding yourself with sin, the farther away you are getting from God!

Imagine we are hiking around in the middle of the wilderness on a mountain top late at night; I am the only one with a flashlight. With no other lights available, in order to see you would need to stay close to me. The farther you walk away from me (and the flashlight) the darker it will get for you. The same thing is true with God. He is the true light of the world. If we want to be able to see the kingdom of heaven clearly, we must get as close as possible to the Light! Get as close as you can to God. The farther away you get from Him, the harder it will be to see the kingdom.

Pray

Work hard at praying, friends. More importantly, make sure to pray consistently. Sometimes people tell me, "I don't know how to pray." If you feel the same way, that's okay! Prayer, like many other things in this world, is something you have to work at and develop over time. You have to practice getting to know God, right? Thus, you have to practice communicating with Him. Finally, if you don't know what to say to Him, say the following words: "God, I don't know what to say to You." Just repeat these words every night until other words come to your mind.

Prayer is a time we dedicate to knowing God—a major step in our spiritual journey. In case you haven't noticed, Christianity has the word *Christ* in it. Hence, *Christianity* means "those who follow Christ." But how can you follow someone you hardly know? Get my drift? Therefore you should set aside a few minutes a day for devotionals. Just put everything away and think about God and focus your mind on your relationship with Him. The more you understand and know Him, the easier your spiritual journey will become.

Challenge #1: Write five things you learned from this book.

Challenge #2: Share this book with a friend.

Discussion Questions

1. What changes do you plan to make in your life after reading this book?
2. What is the biggest thing you learned?
3. What questions do you still have about the Ethiopian Orthodox Tewahedo Church?
4. What kind of Ethiopian Orthodox Tewahedo books would you like to see in the future?
5. Will you recommend this book to others? Why or why not?

FAQ'S for the New Church-Goer

For my dear friends who may still have some questions, I have a gift for you. Here are the most frequently asked questions with their respective answers. I hope you are able to find your question in this list.

How Can I Know If God Exists?

If you are kept up at night wondering if God really exists, just know that you are not alone. Some of the brightest minds have kept their brains busy with this question for thousands of years. To answer this, I have to ask you a question: What does it mean to really know something? Your definition of *know* will dictate your understanding of God. If you want to know God exists by finding some sort of proof, I am sorry to tell you that it's not possible. The Bible instructs us to have faith in God. Paul speaks of faith in this way: "Faith shows the reality of what we hope for; it is the evidence of things we cannot see. Through their faith, the people in days of old earned a good reputation" (Hebrews 11:1–2).

For example, you are reading this book, right? Do you *believe* you are reading this book or do you *know* you are reading this book? You know! Faith is not required here! You can see yourself reading this book, after all. On the other hand, if I told you I originally wrote this book by hand and later typed it on a computer, you would have to believe (or not believe) me. You did not see me writing it. You did not witness the process that went into writing this book. In other words, the things you can see with your eyes do not require faith.

God is invisible. Because of His very nature you are unable to see Him with your eyes, so you cannot prove His existence. At the same time, as you gain knowledge of God your faith grows. Your reasoning to accept His miracles without proof increases. You no longer need to "see" to "see." Do you see?

For example, for every book there is an author. For every computer there is an engineer. For every picture, there is a photographer. Get my drift? Hence, for every universe there has to be something that made it happen. Furthermore, science tells us that before the universe was there was nothing. Last I checked, nothing produces nothing. The universe is something. For something to occur, someone had to create it into being. We call that cause—that creator—God.

How Can I Grow in My Spiritual Life?

There are many similarities between the process of bearing fruit from a seed and growing spiritually. With regard to fruit, five main steps must occur: (1) the soil is cultivated, (2) seed is scattered, (3) the soil is watered and the sun shines, (4) time passes, and (5) the seed bears fruit. Let's see how each of these steps relates to spiritual growth.

The first step in the spiritual journey is to cultivate our hearts (the soil). We must prepare our minds and our hearts to hear the Word of God. We must make a conscious decision to surrender our lives to Jesus Christ. We may not know how to go about it just yet, but the willingness has to be there.

The second step is to receive the Word of God. Much like the seed being scattered, the more we immerse our souls in the Word of God, the more effect it will have on our spiritual success. We must understand that it is the Word of God that has the power to truly change us.

The next step in this journey is to develop the Word of God through our actions. That is how we can "water" the Word of God. Remember: "Faith is dead without good works" (James 2:26). A true Christian is someone who lives by the Word of God.

The final step is arguably the hardest: waiting for the fruit! During this wait our walk must be consistent. Just reading one book or hearing a Christian podcast does not mean our lives will completely change. Neither does it mean we will have a better relationship with God. For us to see substantial results (fruit), we must be willing to allow God to do His part. And as we all know, God works in His time. If you follow all these steps, you will harvest the fruit of your spiritual life!

What Does *Orthodox* Mean?

I'ma drop some knowledge on y'all real quick. This word *orthodox* comes from the Greek word ορθόδοξος (*orthódoxos*), which is composed of the prefix ορθός (*orthós*), meaning "straight, correct, sound" and the suffix δοξα (*doxa*; from the verb δοκέω: "to seem, to think") meaning "belief." When you put the two words together you get the correct (aka ortho) belief (aka dox). Hence, *orthodox* literally means "the correct belief."

Over the years, however, this meaning of the word has changed. *Oxford Dictionary* defines *orthodox* as "following or conforming to the traditional or generally accepted rules or beliefs of a religion, philosophy, or practice." Because of this new meaning, many people associate the orthodoxy, especially in the context of religion, with something that is old school and outdated. Although the old school idea is not necessarily a bad thing, the outdated aspect is completely wrong.

Orthodoxy is the belief that Christ instituted the Church and that His words and teachings are eternal. We believe that Christ had it right (aka ορθός = correct) 2,000 years ago, and we human beings who are subject to error should not try to reform and update His teachings. I don't know if you noticed, but everything we do at an Orthodox Church is extremely old school. This is because of the way things were done two thousand years ago. If Christ taught His disciples to conduct church in a particular way (aka δοξα = belief), who are we to change His teaching today? So *orthodoxy* is the ability to resist any change that can come to the teachings of Christ.

Where Can I Get an Ethiopian Orthodox Bible?

Sorry, Boo-Boo. There is no such thing. A Bible is a Bible. The Ethiopian Orthodox Church uses the same Bible other denominations use. Take a minute or two to compose yourself because I know this probably blew your mind. 😊

Let's take a second to understand what the Bible is. The word *bible*, like many English words, is derived from the Greek τὰ βιβλία (*ta biblia*), meaning "books." Hence, *Bible* simply means "a collection of books." That is why we say the *book* of Genesis, Exodus, Leviticus, and so on. Interestingly enough, until about the fourth century these were considered to be individual books. Wouldn't you know it? Someone had the bright idea to put all these books together for people's convenience—but more importantly, to bring people into agreement as to which books are considered to be inspired by God and which books are not.

This step was important because many people were falsely spreading around "holy" books to early Christians. These books contradicted the teachings of Christ. Therefore, it was important to decide which books should be included in the final count and which books should not be. This part is a little tricky: After a series of complicated events, the Ethiopian Orthodox Church ended up "accepting" 46 books in the Old Testament and 35 books in the New Testament, a grand total of 81 books of the Bible. To put this in perspective, the Catholic Church accepts 73 books; most of the world uses the Bible that includes 66 books. Thus, if you have a Bible that has 66 books out of the 81, it is still a Bible. On the other hand, if you are looking for a Bible that includes all 81 books that the Ethiopian Orthodox Church accepts, you won't find it. As of the writing of this book, none exist. Most of the additional books are lengthy and it would be inconvenient to try to publish all the books together. Therefore, any Bible with 66 books will do!

Why Should I Read the Bible?

You should read the Bible because the entire book is about you! Most people assume that the Bible is about Jesus, but it's really not. Yes, Jesus plays a major role in the Bible, but if this were a movie, He would be a supporting actor. You are the center main character of the entire book. In summary, the Old Testament talks about how God created you and loved you. But this fairytale story is cut short when you become seriously sick and are diagnosed with a horrible disease known as sin.

The rest of the Old Testament describes how you do your very best to heal yourself by trying various things but ultimately are unable to. Just when you are about to give up hope, you enter the New Testament. God hears your cries and sends you the best medicine known to mankind: Jesus Christ. Jesus proves Himself to be the best medicine and offers Himself to you. The Bible ends with Jesus, the only medicine that can heal you, being offered to you. You are now left with a decision to accept this medicine or to deny Him.

What Parts of the Bible Should I Read First? Can I Skip Around?

Perhaps the most common mistake I see when people read the Bible for the first time is starting from chapter 1 of Genesis and trying to read straight through to Revelation. If it is your first time reading the Bible, I can promise you that you will not make it past Exodus (the second book of the Bible) if you begin this way. There are strategies you can use, however. Let's take a look.

The first thing you have to determine is what are you hoping to get from the Bible. For example, if you are seeking advice from God, books like Proverbs and the Wisdom of Solomon are a great place to start. When you are trying to pray using the Bible, Psalms is the place to go.

When trying to strengthen your relationship with Christ, you should start by reading the Gospels (Matthew, Mark, Luke, and John). If you just want to understand the historical aspect of the Bible, read books like 1 and 2 Samuel or the book of Acts. There are also numerous Bible reading apps available that will guide you to a section to read on a specified day. Finally, some Bibles have a topic index. Check that out too.

Don't get me wrong—the Bible is an integrated book and deserves to be read in its entirety. The thing about it is this: if you keep on starting from Genesis 1:1 and find yourself unable to get through it all, it is time to try something different.

Which Version of the Bible Should I Read?

Various versions of the Bible are a result of the methods used by scholars to translate the Bible from Greek and Hebrew into English. As you can imagine, there are various ways to go about translating words. For example, if you happen to speak Amharic, you may have considered how to translate the phrase "What's up?" እንዴት አደርክ? (ʾənədetə ʾädärəkə). The most literal translation to the phrase "What's up?" however, would be: ምንድን ነው ወዳላይ (mənədənə näwə wädälayə), which would mean something like "What direction is above my head?" You see the issue? The English phrase is a greeting; you are stuck with trying to translate each text as literally as possible, but in the midst of doing that, you can easily lose the spirit of the text. Scholars face the same type of difficulty as they translate the Bible, especially when working with subject matters as intricate and delicate as those in the Word of God. Therefore, you must consider the two different approaches: literal translations versus most accurate meanings. The choice results in various versions of the Bible. Which one should you use?

Like many things in life, it all depends, my friend! If you keep hearing about a dude named Abraham or Isaac and you want to know more about them, you can use any version of the Bible you wish in order to understand the historical background. If you are using the Bible as a means to connect to God and to accompany your prayers, simply get a Bible you can understand. I often see young kids using an older English version of the Bible that even Shakespeare would have not been able to understand. The Bible is meant to be read and understood! On the other hand, if you are reading the Bible to understand the mystical teachings of the church, like dogmatic matters, I would say that the English language is simply not good enough. This is why our church still uses Ge'ez. Even here in America no serious theologians read the Bible in English. They instead retreat to Greek or Hebrew because of how weak the English language is. (More on the English language later.)

Where Can I Get a Confession Father?

Ideally, your confession father should be someone at your local church. His job is to monitor your spiritual growth as you continue to come to the church. Over the years there have been serious questions about not being able to confess to a confession father because of the language barrier. I would strongly suggest that you at least try to talk with the priests at your local church first. See if there are ways that you will be able to communicate. Don't just assume that your priest will not be able to understand you. Your priest can be more understanding than you may think. If you cannot find an English-speaking priest at your local church, try to search for others in other churches. This includes all the sister churches with whom we are in full communion: the Eritrean-Orthodox Church, Coptic Orthodox Church, Armenian Orthodox Church, Malankara (often referred to as Indian) Orthodox Church, and Syriac Orthodox Church. You can go to any one of the churches and talk to an English-speaking priest and confess to him.

Why Do Females Have to Wear *Netelas* to Church?

Consider the following scripture:

> I am so glad that you always keep me in your thoughts, and that you are following the teachings I passed on to you. But there is one thing I want you to know: The head of every man is Christ, the head of woman is man, and the head of Christ is God. A man dishonors his head if he covers his head while praying or prophesying. But a woman dishonors her head if she prays or prophesies without a covering on her head, for this is the same as shaving her head. Yes, if she refuses to wear a head covering, she should cut off all her hair! But since it is shameful for a woman to have her hair cut or her head shaved, she should wear a covering. (1 Corinthians 11:2–6)

Covering the head, as seen above, is something Paul instructed women to do, especially during prayer. But why are the *netelas* white? We see the answer in Psalm 51:7: "Cleanse me with hyssop, and I will be clean; wash me, and I will be whiter than snow" (NIV). Thus, the white symbolizes our desire to be clean of sin. Furthermore, we wish to be sitting one day next to the "armies of heaven . . . following him, riding on white horses and dressed in fine linen, white and clean" (Revelation 19:14 NIV).

Why Can't Females Become Priests?

The reason females cannot become priests is found in the 1 Timothy 2:12: "I do not permit a woman to teach or to assume authority over a man; she must be quiet" (NIV). Dear brothers and sisters in Christ, please do not dismiss the above verse as being a statement simply reflecting the ideology of Paul's time. Even a novice Bible reader would recognize that most of Christ's teachings directly challenged the culture and ideology that existed at the time. If Christ or His disciples wished for women to join the priesthood, there would have been a clear teaching giving permission for women to be priestesses. Contrary to modern-day belief, neighboring cities of the Israelites employed priestesses (female priests); hence, the culture *would* have been accepting to the idea of women becoming priests. Despite the cultural acceptance, however, the Bible prohibited women from becoming priests. Why? Allow me to digress for a brief moment . . .

If you were a Hollywood director, would you hire a woman or a man to play the role of Christ? I think the answer is clear. Now the priest, especially during the services of liturgy, is playing the role of Christ. In fact, the whole liturgy service not only chronicles the life of Christ, but through faith we believe the events of Christ are taking place before our eyes! If even the secular world of Hollywood can be cautious enough to select only men to play the role of Christ to make the movie as realistic as possible, how much more cautious should Christians be?

Why Do We Fast?

Consider the words of Jesus in Mark 9:29: "So He said to them, 'This kind can come out by nothing but prayer and fasting'" (NKJV). Fasting is the act of restricting oneself from something that is desired. It is a tool, much like prayer, that we use to correct ourselves. If done correctly, fasting can benefit both the flesh and the soul.

With regard to the flesh, it is safe to say that everyone fasts (restricts himself or herself) to some degree from unhealthy food. Because the Ethiopian Orthodox Tewahedo Church requires that we abstain from dairy, meat products, and alcoholic beverages (which if not restricted can become deleterious) during fasting periods, our flesh benefits from fasting!

Regarding the soul, the money we would have been spending on the foods we are restricted from should be spent on the poor, as the gospel requires. Furthermore, when the flesh becomes weak the soul is strengthened, for the two are in constant battle with each other. For the flesh lusts against the Spirit, and the Spirit against the flesh; the flesh can prevent us from doing the right things we want to do unless we submit to the Spirit (Galatians 5:17).

Why Do People Incorporate Saints into Their Prayers?

> "He who receives a prophet in the name of a prophet shall receive a prophet's reward. And he who receives a righteous man in the name of

a righteous man shall receive a righteous man's reward. And whoever gives one of these little ones only a cup of cold water in the name of a disciple, assuredly, I say to you, he shall by no means lose his reward." (Matthew 10:41–42 NKJV)

The first misconception we have to clear up is this: contrary to popular thought, we worship a God who is already honored! The notion that "we take away from God's glory by asking for the saints' intercession" is at best blasphemous. God's glory is not something that can be "taken away." Second, as the verses above indicate, honoring and prostrating (*sigdet*) to saints and angels is something the Bible permits. Below we see just a few examples from the Bible about prostration to God as well as to saints and angels.

Prostration to God

So Moses and Aaron went from the presence of the assembly to the door of the tabernacle of meeting, and they fell on their faces. And the glory of the Lord appeared to them. (Numbers 20:6 NKJV)

Oh come, let us worship and bow down;
Let us kneel before the Lord our Maker.
For He is our God. (Psalm 95:6–7 NKJV)

Prostration to Angels and Saints

Now the two angels came to Sodom in the evening, and Lot was sitting in the gate of Sodom. When Lot saw them, he rose to meet them, and he bowed himself with his face toward the ground. (Genesis 19:1 NKJV)

So it was, when he came to David, that he fell to

> the ground and prostrated himself. (2 Samuel 1:2 NKJV)

> Then David said to all the assembly, "Now bless the Lord your God." So all the assembly blessed the Lord God of their fathers, and bowed their heads and prostrated themselves before the Lord and the king. (1 Chronicles 29:20 NKJV)

It is clear from the verses above that there are two distinct forms of honoring and prostrating. One is reserved solely for our Creator, while the second is a show of respect we give to saints and angels. We incorporate saints and angels into our prayers because we believe they intercede for us to God. That by no means prevents us from praying directly to God.

Let's ponder the following question for a second: Have you ever asked a friend to pray for you? Well, that is by definition asking for someone's intercession. Instead of asking the average man, who is still distracted by the sinful nature of this world, to pray for you, why not ask the saints, who are not distracted? Furthermore, have you ever read an article or heard a testimony about a pastor or someone within a Christian community for inspiration? What more inspiration can we have than the stories of those saints who have already defeated the desires of their flesh? Since their stories are inspiring, we commemorate the saints and angels on a specific day so we may never forget of the great works they did. Before we conclude this discussion, however, let us look at biblical support for the subject of intercession in case any doubt remains.

> Therefore I exhort first of all that supplications, prayers, intercessions, and giving of thanks be

made for all men, for kings and all who are in authority, that we may lead a quiet and peaceable life in all godliness and reverence. (1 Timothy 2:1–2 NKJV)

Is anyone among you sick? Let him call for the elders of the church, and let them pray over him, anointing him with oil in the name of the Lord. (James 5:14 NKJV)

Therefore the people came to Moses, and said, "We have sinned, for we have spoken against the Lord and against you; pray to the Lord that He take away the serpents from us." So Moses prayed for the people. (Numbers 21:7 NKJV)

Finally, brethren, pray for us, that the word of the Lord may run swiftly and be glorified, just as it is with you. (2 Thessalonians 3:1 NKJV)

Why Do We Have Icons and Why Do We Pray Looking at Them?

Let us look at the book of Exodus as a basis for why we should not have images within the church.

> "You shall make a veil woven of blue, purple, and scarlet thread, and fine woven linen. It shall be woven with an artistic design of cherubim. You shall hang it upon the four pillars of acacia wood overlaid with gold. Their hooks shall be gold, upon four sockets of silver." (Exodus 26:31–32 NKJV)

Interestingly enough, people mistakenly reference the following commandment when they speak against using icons in the church:

> "You shall not make for yourself a carved image—any likeness of anything that is in heaven above, or that is in the earth beneath, or that is in the water under the earth." (Exodus 20:4 NKJV)

However, when read in context we realize that the people who existed at that time would carve images of gods and worship the images. The images in the Ethiopian Orthodox Tewahedo Church are *not* being worshiped. Instead, the images help devout Christians during worship. For example, heaven forbid, but if you found yourselves separated from a loved one—oh, let's say from your father—a picture would help you remember him but not replace him. In the same way, when we see a picture of our Heavenly Father we are reminded of the great sacrifice the Son had to endure for our salvation. In addition, as you are reading this very sentence a certain image will pop into your head if I say the word *Bible*. That's because individual letters of the alphabet when organized in a certain order convey information to our heads. This information causes our brains to be activated; in turn, the mind produces images in our heads. Therefore, letters in retrospect are forms of images!

The Bible gives us the accounts of events that occurred before, during, and after the life of Christ. While we read the accounts, our brains create images of their own. Realizing this, our Church permitted icons to be employed because, much like the Bible, the icons tell us a story about events that occurred before, during, and after the life of Christ. Finally, just as we give certain respect to the Bible because it tells us a story about those we respect, we give respect to the icons because they hold the image of those we respect.

What Exactly Is *Itan (Incense)* and Why Is It Incorporated into Our Liturgy?

> Let my prayer be set before You as incense, The lifting up of my hands as the evening sacrifice. (Psalm 141:2 NKJV)

During the liturgy and at other times of prayer, priests use a censer to perfume the church with the beautiful scent of incense. God instructed Moses how to make the censer and the incense (see Exodus 30), and incense is offered as a sacrifice before God for the atonement of sins. When Israel sinned before God and was struck with a plague, Aaron the priest offered incense for their sins and the plague stopped (see Numbers 16:46–50). We believe that prayers ascend toward heaven in the smoke of the incense.

The censer is the altar that is used to burn the incense. It has three chains on the sides and one in the middle that holds the other three together. This is a symbol of the Holy Trinity (Three Persons=Father, Son, Holy Spirit=One God). The round part where the incense is placed represents the womb of the virgin Mary, and the fire represents the divinity of Christ. Just as the fire does not burn the censer, the virgin Mary bore God in her womb without being burned by the fire of His divinity.

The use of the censer and incense is not an outdated tradition. For example, in the following scripture you can see that incense is used even by the angels in heaven to worship God:

> Then another angel, having a golden censer, came and stood at the altar. He was given much incense, that he should offer it with the prayers of all the saints upon the golden altar which was

before the throne. And the smoke of the incense, with the prayers of the saints, ascended before God from the angel's hand. (Revelation 8:3–4 NKJV)

What Are the Structure and Hierarchy of Our Clergy and How Do They Connect to the Bible?

Regardless of how modern society feels about priests, the truth is that Jesus gave them the authority to forgive sins.

> Then he breathed on them and said, "Receive the Holy Spirit. If you forgive anyone's sins, they are forgiven. If you do not forgive them, they are not forgiven." (John 20:22–23)

Christ had chosen these apostles—this right was not given to everyone. For example, we see in the book of Luke that Jesus "called his disciples to him and chose . . . them" (6:13 NIV). Within the Ethiopian Orthodox Tehwhedo Church there are three ranks for clergy:

Deacons

> Likewise deacons must be reverent, not double-tongued, not given to much wine, not greedy for money, holding the mystery of the faith with a pure conscience. But let these also first be tested; then let them serve as deacons, being found blameless. (1 Timothy 3:8–10 NKJV)

Priests

> "For the lips of a priest should keep knowledge, And people should seek the law from his mouth; For he is the messenger of the Lord of hosts." (Malachi 2:7 NKJV)

Bishops

> For a bishop must be blameless, as a steward of God, not self-willed, not quick-tempered, not given to wine, not violent, not greedy for money, but hospitable, a lover of what is good, sober-minded, just, holy, self-controlled, holding fast the faithful word as he has been taught, that he may be able, by sound doctrine, both to exhort and convict those who contradict. (Titus 1:7–9 NKJV)

Why Do We Take Off Our Shoes When We Come into the Church?

In Exodus 3:5 we are told to "take your sandals off your feet, for the place where you stand is holy ground" (NKJV). Now I'm sure you remember getting that popular shoe brand you always wanted. Oh, how you promised yourself the care you would give that special pair of shoes! But eventually the once-clean and new shoes slowly became dirty and old. Why? When we use our shoes to walk around in this world, they inevitably pick up dirt and thus become dirty. In the same sense, when we were born we were new and clean. As we kept living in this world, however, our hearts began to accumulate the dirt of this world (adultery, fornication, uncleanness, lewdness, idolatry, sorcery, hatred, contentions, jealousies, outbursts of wrath, selfishness, ambitions, dissensions, heresies, envy, murders, drunkenness, revelries, and so on). When we walk into a church, we do not wish to bring any dirt of the world to the holy and sanctified sanctuary. Thus, by taking off our shoes we remind ourselves to also take off the "shoes" of our hearts, which have been inundated by the filth of this world.

Why Do We Baptize Infants?

We are told in the John 3:5 that "no one can enter the Kingdom of God without being born of water and the Spirit." Notice that the verse explicitly states "no one" can enter the Kingdom of God without being baptized. It does not say "adults" or "parents." It is clear: "no one" without qualification.

So what will happen to innocent children, heaven forbid, if they depart from this world without being baptized? Consider the following:

> One day some parents brought their children to Jesus so he could lay his hands on them and pray for them. But the disciples scolded the parents for bothering him. But Jesus said, "Let the children come to me. Don't stop them! For the Kingdom of Heaven belongs to those who are like these children." (Matthew 19:13–14)

Dear brothers and sisters, we are also forced to recall what God ordered Abraham in Genesis:

> "You must cut off the flesh of your foreskin as a sign of the covenant between me and you. From generation to generation, every male child must be circumcised on the eighth day after his birth. This applies not only to members of your family but also to the servants born in your household and the foreign-born servants whom you have purchased." (Genesis 17:11–12)

In the Old Testament the sign for the covenant made between God and man was circumcision. In the New Testament the sign is baptism. Because God Himself ordered men of Abraham's descendants to get the sign of the covenant as infants, we are not in a position to forbid infants of the New Testament to get the sign of the covenant, which is now baptism.

Why Do Boys Get Baptized at Forty Days Old and Girls at Eighty?

Boys: 7 days (unclean) + 33 days (purification days) = 40 days

> Then the Lord spoke to Moses, saying, "Speak to the children of Israel, saying: 'If a woman has conceived, and borne a male child, then she shall be unclean seven days; as in the days of her customary impurity she shall be unclean. And on the eighth day the flesh of his foreskin shall be circumcised. She shall then continue in the blood of her purification thirty-three days. She shall not touch any hallowed thing, nor come into the sanctuary until the days of her purification are fulfilled.'" (Leviticus 12: 1–4 NKJV)

Girls: 14 days (unclean) + 66 days (purification days) = 80 days

> "'But if she bears a female child, then she shall be unclean two weeks, as in her customary impurity, and she shall continue in the blood of her purification sixty-six days.'" (Leviticus 12: 5 NKJV)

Why Do We Use the *Geez* Language During Services?

> Come, let Us go down and there confuse their language, that they may not understand one another's speech. (Genesis 11:7 NKJV)

Let us do a quick review of English grammar, focusing on the usage of the verb *come* (see Table 1) in the second person.

	Singular	Plural
Second Person M	**come**	**come**
Second Person F	**come**	**come**

Table 1: English Verb *Come*   Key: M = Masculine; F = Feminine

Genesis 11:7 teaches us about the Triune God. Although the subject of the Trinity is not within the scope of this discussion, we know that when God said, "Come, let Us go down," He was revealing His triune nature. Now here is the point: just from this verse alone we can determine how many persons there are. Referring back to Table 1, the verb *come* is used for second person in both the singular and plural case. Hence, we know from this verse that there are *at least* two persons (the person talking and the person(s) He is talking to).

Let us look into the Amharic version:

ኑ፥ እንውረድ፤ አንዱ የአንዱን ነገር እንዳይሰማው ቋንቋቸውን በዚያ እንደባልቀው፡፡ ኦሪት ዘፍጥረት 11:7

Now, let us review the Amharic Grahamar for its usage of the verb ና (to come):

	Singular	Plural
Second Person M	ና	ኑ
Second Person F	ነይ	ኑ

Table 2: Amharic verb "ና"[27]   Key: M = Masculine; F = Feminine

---

27   Genesis 11:7 is *not* the only verse the Church relies upon to teach us about the triune nature of God. There are many more

The Amharic version uses the plural version ኑ. This indicates that the person speaking was talking to at least two more persons, bringing the total to at least three persons: the person talking plus at least two persons he was talking to). We know that the Triune God is three persons, so the Amharic version gives us a better idea of the nature of God.

It is also important to mention that the Geez provides a richer description by discerning between masculine and feminine verbs in the plural case. The point is this: English by its very nature is a weak language because most of the root words go back to a different language (Greek, Latin, and so on). Amharic, although better than English, is also derived from Geez; hence, one cannot truly understand Amharic without understanding Geez.

Finally, the Geez root word is *Geez*! Since the New Testament books translated as early as the fifth century were in Geez, one does not need to search another language's root word to understand the meaning of a particular passage. Moreover, as seen above, the language in itself is stronger and better suited to describe the nature of God. Therefore, the Church is still employing the Geez language during services.

---

verses that accurately describe the three persons of the Triune God.

Resources[28]

YOUNG ORTHODOX TEWAHEDO CHURCH [YOTC]

YOTC's mission is to connect members to Christ by delivering the authentic message of salvation in English while adhering to the EOTC doctrine, canon, and tradition. Through various services, YOTC aims to bring young adults closer to the Church and ensure spiritual growth for devious Christians while providing an inclusive environment.

YOTC Resources

- *YOTC.org:* Our official web site, which has plenty of resources to include prayers, books, video sermons, current YOTC events, and so much more.

- Sunday Afternoon Class: YOTC holds weekly Sunday afternoon classes on various topics such as the Five Pillars of Mystery, the Seven Sacraments, Early Church History, the Divine Liturgy, and so much more. Please visit YOTC's *YouTube* page (Young OTC) to learn more.

- English Hymn (*mezmur*) CD: Search for "The Nation of the Cross" on *iTunes* or *Spotify* to download the music.

---

[28] All resource information except "Proverbs 31 Squad" taken from the following websites: yotc.org, uoty.org, and stsa.church.

- English Service: YOTC aims to hold English services quarterly based on relevant topics.

- *Instagram* and *Facebook*: Follow our social media pages to stay current on our various services (*Instagram*: YoungOTC; *Facebook*: Young Orthodox Tewahedo Christians).

- *YouTube*: Young OTC.

If you are in the Washington, D.C., area, please be sure to attend and check out the various programs YOTC has to offer by contacting us at contactus@yotc.org.

UNITED ORTHODOX TEWAHEDO YOUTH [UOTY]

Mission

Our mission is to unite youth groups of Ethiopian and non-Ethiopian descent who reside in North America for a common spiritual cause and deliver the authentic message of salvation in English while adhering to the doctrine, dogma, canon, and sacred tradition of the Ethiopian Orthodox Tewahedo Church.

Purpose

The purpose of this group is to break the language barrier that is currently keeping Ethiopian-American youth away from the Church of their forefathers by conducting services in English. The group will also sponsor spiritual conferences, and foster networking platforms throughout North America.

For more info. please visit uoty.org or email uoty.pr@gmail.com.

RESOURCES

SAINT TIMOTHY AND SAINT ATHANASIUS COPTIC ORTHODOX CHURCH [STSA]

Who

Saint Timothy and Saint Athanasius Coptic Orthodox Church [STSA] was founded in Arlington, Virginia, in 2012 with the vision of bringing an ancient faith to a modern world. It presents eternal truths that have been around for two thousand years in a way that's real and relevant to modern culture. It is a place where people can unite to worship God as one family—regardless of ethnic, cultural, or spiritual background.

How

STSA brings an ancient faith to a modern world by encouraging and equipping people to passionately pursue God through life and learning groups, experience transformational worship through the liturgy, build authentic community in leisure groups and events, and influence the world around them through volunteering and with powerful messages.

Sunday Services

Each Sunday we hold two services, a liturgical worship service followed by The Well, a service with uplifting music and an inspiring, relevant message. The children and youth programs are also held during this time. Everyone is welcome to join any Sunday.

For more info. visit on the web at *stsa.church* or write at the following address:

>George Mason University
>Van Metre Hall (Room 125)
>3351 Fairfax Drive
>Arlington, VA 22201

PROVERBS 31 SQUAD

Purpose

Proverbs 31 Squad has a mission to better understand the roles and powers women have within the Ethiopian Orthodox Tewahedo Church. This group hosts monthly calls in which a lesson is given about biblical women who are examples of the ideal Proverbs 31 "virtuous" woman. Then a discussion follows on how the lesson can be relatable in the daily lives of Christian women through practical monthly assignments that are given.

For more info please follow *@proverbs31squad* on *Instagram*.

RECOMMENDED BOOKS

Life of Repentance and Purity (Saint Vladimir's Seminary Press), by Pope Shenouda III

> This is one of the many books written by Pope Shenouda III. It is an extremely valuable resource for understanding what repentance means.

The Love Chapter: The Meaning of First Corinthians 13 (Paraclete Press), by Saint John Chrysostom

> Do you want to have deeper understanding about what true love means from a biblical point of view? This commentary is helpful in improving our relationships with others and applying true love in our lives.

RESOURCES

"WHATEVER, GOD": Rediscovering the One I Thought I Knew (Xulon Press), by Fr. Anthony Messeh

Too many people stumble through life with an inaccurate view of who God is. They believe in His existence but don't know how to relate to Him in a practical and meaningful way. As a result, they fail to achieve anything beyond a superficial relationship with their Creator and live less-than-fulfilling lives. In *"WHATEVER, GOD,"* Fr. Anthony Messeh attempts to change that. He shares his unique story and the lessons he's learned that helped him go from a "don't-get-too-close-to-God-because-He-might-ruin-your-life" Christian to a fully devoted "I-can't-get-enough-of-God-in-my-life" believer.

For He who has inspired me to begin, who helped me begin and finish, for the magnificent God, may all glory be given to Him.

Made in the USA
Middletown, DE
23 December 2019